Science and the Sacred

Science *and the* Sacred

Beyond the Gods in Our Image

C.S. Pearce
and Philip Clayton

CASCADE *Books* · Eugene, Oregon

SCIENCE AND THE SACRED
Beyond the Gods in Our Image

Copyright © 2025 C.S. Pearce and Philip Clayton. All rights reserved. Except for brief quotations in critical publications or reviews, no part of this book may be reproduced in any manner without prior written permission from the publisher. Write: Permissions, Wipf and Stock Publishers, 199 W. 8th Ave., Suite 3, Eugene, OR 97401.

Cascade Books
An Imprint of Wipf and Stock Publishers
199 W. 8th Ave., Suite 3
Eugene, OR 97401

www.wipfandstock.com

PAPERBACK ISBN: 978-1-6667-6995-1
HARDCOVER ISBN: 978-1-6667-6996-8
EBOOK ISBN: 978-1-6667-6997-5

Cataloguing-in-Publication data:

Names: Pearce, C. S., author. | Clayton, Philip, 1956–, author.

Title: Science and the sacred : beyond the gods in our image / C.S. Pearce and Philip Clayton.

Description: Eugene, OR: Cascade Books, 2025. | Includes bibliographical references.

Identifiers: ISBN 978-1-6667-6995-1 (paperback) | ISBN 978-1-6667-6996-8 (hardcover) | ISBN 978-1-6667-6997-5 (ebook)

Subjects: LCSH: Science and religion. | Process theology. | Evolution—Religious aspects.

Classification: BL241.P43.2025 (print). | BL241 (ebook).

Scripture quotations marked (NLT) are taken from the *Holy Bible*, New Living Translation, copyright ©1996, 2004, 2015 by Tyndale House Foundation. Used by permission of Tyndale House Publishers, Carol Stream, Illinois 60188. All rights reserved.

VERSION NUMBER 02/06/25

Contents

Preface | vii

Part One: Creation: What We Now Know | 1

1. In Search of the Sacred | 3
2. In the Beginning... | 9
3. We Are All Star-Stuff | 13
   Cosmology and Astrophysics: An Existential Summary of Chapter 3 | 25
4. The Dynamic Drive at Life's Core | 27
   Biology and Evolution: An Existential Summary of Chapter 4 | 39
5. Our Big Brains & Why We Are the Way We Are | 43
   Neuroscience: An Existential Summary of Chapter 5 | 58

Part Two: Religion Comes of Age | 61

6. An Omnipresent God | 63
7. Religion Comes of Age | 80
   Religion and the Sacred: An Existential Summary of Chapter 7 | 87
8. A Way to Hold Both Your Faith and Your Doubts | 89
9. Holy Books and Miracles | 99
10. The Afterlife | 116

Contents

11 Science, Religion, and Sacred Stories | 123

12 Our Sacred Story: Two Visions | 137

13 Conclusion: Now What? | 149

Appendix A: Creative Emergence or Intelligent Design? | 153
Appendix B: What About Miracles? | 169
Endnotes | 177

Preface

WE, THE AUTHORS, HAVE long been fascinated by, and struggled with, issues of faith, science, and human nature. Although we've arrived at a similar understanding of these issues, we each traveled very different paths in life to get here. We also differ in our places on the atheism-to-theism spectrum, with one of us using the label atheist and the other theist. Instead of approaching our differences with animosity and distrust, we have explored them with curiosity, discovering far more similarities than differences.

In this book, we affirm the basic truth that the major scientific breakthroughs of our era offer better opportunities for enlightenment, wisdom, insight, and integration than were possible in previous eras. Thanks to these breakthroughs, we can now think about ultimate concerns in new, more open and courageous ways—ways that can dramatically increase our understanding of why we are the way we are, and that better equip us to work together for the common good.

We invite readers of all faiths and of no faith to join us on a journey through these new ways of thinking and the awe-inspiring discoveries that have made them possible. The journey may be uncomfortable for some, and so we begin with this brief introduction, so that those who are about to join us know who we are and why we are making this invitation.

Philip Clayton, Ingraham Professor at Claremont School of Theology (CST), has taught and written for several decades on the relations between religion, science, and theology. He has helped organize research groups and

Preface

conferences on these issues on five continents, working with the Vatican, the British Council, Harvard University, and many others. He has published and lectured extensively on these subjects for both academic audiences and the general public, including interviews on National Public Radio, BBC programs, and Caltech's Athenaeum, and is the author or editor of some two dozen books, including *The Oxford Handbook of Religion and Science*.

Although his entire career has been academic, most recently he has branched out to head EcoCiv.org, an organization that works with allies and global leaders to design solutions for the well-being of people and the planet, because he believes climate change is the most critical challenge facing humanity today. In that capacity he has led symposia through the physics department at the University of California, Berkeley and Harvard's Center for the Environment, and moderated panels for COP26, the United Nations' Global Climate Summit, in Glasgow in 2021. He also edited *The New Possible: Visions of our World Beyond Crisis* (Cascade Books, 2021), which offers an inspiring roadmap for action with twenty-eight unique visions of what could be, assembled from global leaders on six continents. Most recently he delivered the James Gregory Lectures on Science, Religion and Human Flourishing at Edinburgh and St Andrews Universities in the UK.

Clayton has received a Fulbright Fellowship, an Alexander von Humboldt Professorship, and the Templeton Research Prize and Templeton Book Prize, among many other honors. Prior to joining the faculty at CST, Clayton taught or held research professorships at Williams College, California State University, Harvard University, Cambridge University, and the University of Munich. He holds a joint PhD from the Religious Studies and Philosophy departments at Yale University.

C. S. Pearce is a writer whose work has been published in the *Los Angeles Times*, the *Washington Post*, and other media. She served five years as director of media relations for CST, a position she accepted just as the school was about to launch its graduate program, in which ministers, rabbis, imams, leaders in the Dharma faiths, and atheists were educated side by side, with some of their classes in common. Everyone involved felt that this kind of cooperation was critical for a world struggling with religiously motivated violence and alienation. She helped the school gain national and international attention for its new programs.

In 2012, while still at CST, she wrote *This We Believe: The Christian Case for Gay Civil Rights*, which was a finalist for the American Library

Preface

Association's Stonewall Book Awards. Prior to that, she wrote books and magazine articles for the San Diego Zoological Society (her most popular book sold ninety thousand copies), and articles for San Diego's NPR and PBS station, KPBS. She has interviewed secular, religious, and arts leaders, as well as scientists, activists, and environmentalists. Her many writing honors include the Media Award from the National Conference for Community and Justice and magazine story of the year awards from San Diego's Gay & Lesbian Alliance Against Defamation.

Before becoming a writer, she was a computer programmer and systems analyst for twelve years, and then joined her husband on a one and a half year service mission in the Dominican Republic—he gave medical care to the destitute, and she assisted resourceful individuals who had begun microindustries. She received a BA in mathematics from the University of California, Irvine; and an MBA from the University of Michigan, Ann Arbor; and she undertook her journalism education at San Diego State University when she switched careers.

For both of us, acknowledging the beauty and complexity of our cosmic and earthly origins has been an exhilarating and uplifting part of our spiritual experience. We believe that the world would be better off if more people had a realistic understanding of our origins and creation, and this book is our attempt to help make that happen. So, whoever you are and wherever you find yourself on this path called life, welcome! Please join us as we explore new ways to look at the ultimate issues of being, meaning, purpose, and the common good.

Part One

Creation: What We Now Know

"God did something much more clever than create a clockwork world. God created a world that could make itself."

—Krista Tippett, journalist and host of
On Being with Krista Tippett

1

In Search of the Sacred

FOR THOUSANDS OF YEARS, religion offered humanity an ordered universe and the answers to its ultimate questions. It gave us a sense of the sublime that, at its best, inspired art and beauty, love and altruism, and a vision of a better world.

Yet religion has had a tribal and toxic side as well, a side that still flourishes, even in the supposedly enlightened West. Some of our cocitizens follow a supernatural God who intervenes in the world in arbitrary ways, a God whom many today find hard to accept.

It is no secret that the older notions of God are losing their hold on many, especially in the younger generations. To their ears, the words of the loudest religious leaders often seem heartless and ignorant; denial of verified science is ruining God's reputation. Moreover, as our understanding of ethics and reality has expanded, the cognitive dissonance of believing in a God who is all-powerful *and* all-good has increased; there's just too much suffering in this world.

As a result, many today now regard religion as regressive, with decreasing credibility, and God as irrelevant or worse. Even people of faith struggle with such doubts, and the ranks of the religiously unaffiliated are soaring. What's more, when believers ask their spiritual leaders for help with their doubts and struggles, too often they are told to just relax and take traditional beliefs on faith because it is all a mystery. Or they are encouraged to reject modern science in favor of alternative views of the natural world that lack empirical support.

Part One: Creation: What We Now Know

The plunging membership of Western churches, synagogues, and mosques over the past few decades suggests that the denials of science and religious pluralism aren't working—not for laypeople, and not for an increasing number of their religious leaders. Most progressive clerics and rabbis have openly acknowledged the reality of these dilemmas for some time now, but more recently these issues have been affecting the more traditional and fundamentalist denominations as well. In the Christian tradition, an increasing number of conservative and evangelical pastors are having a crisis of faith because they have trouble believing in the God their tradition proclaims. Because they have studied the biblical and theological issues in greater depth than their congregations have, they realize that much of the "old, old story" doesn't quite hold up.[1]

And yet . . . many of these same people—questioning believers, doubters, cynics, and skeptics alike—are still open to the transcendent and oriented to a sense of gratitude toward something larger than themselves. Science and nature, they realize, are providing revelations of their own that create a deep and abiding sense of awe when we take the time to pay attention. Yet when we attempt to rebuild the sacred from the rubble of an anthropomorphic God overlaid with a veneer of the latest science, it doesn't seem to work very well. So . . . *Now what?*

We, the authors, wrote this book because we believe that a renewed concept of the sacred is not just possible, it is imperative. The definition of "sacred" must be enlarged, and, for that matter, so must our understanding of "spirituality."

Traditionally both of these words have been connected with religion and the worship of God, the gods, or the supernatural. Many of our atheist friends dislike them for that reason. There are, however, no good secular equivalents for "the sacred" and "spirituality," even though secular people most certainly experience the feelings and emotions that these two words encompass.

Therefore, in the book, we use expanded definitions of what is sacred and what is spiritual that include everyone: believers, agnostics, atheists, and even those who don't really think much about ultimate questions.

No religion or nonreligion has a monopoly on human experience, and the emotions connected with sacredness and spirituality are real and true for each one of us. They are also deeply subjective, in that what we conclude they mean depends on our individual belief system and personality.

In other words, although our subjective experiences are true and real for each one of us, what they cause us to believe about verifiable facts—science, the universe, and even the experiences themselves—may not be accurate. So, when a patient tells his doctor that God healed him, for example, his doctor may know that it was the antibiotics she prescribed, not a supernatural intervention. But this does not invalidate the patient's experience of awe and gratitude at being cured.

For this reason, we propose the following expanded definitions of "sacred" and "spirituality" that include secular and religious worldviews:

Sacred: Something profound, worthy of special regard, that inspires wonder, awe, and reverence; anything that helps increase our interconnectedness.

Spirituality: Practices (such as meditation, prayer, ecstatic dancing, the study of the cosmos) and deeply felt experiences (in nature, music, art, literature, and the different kinds of love) that enable us to transcend our everyday consciousness and feel peace and connection to something larger than ourselves. Spirituality often involves a search for meaning and purpose and informs the deepest values and meanings by which we live.

Such expanded definitions are becoming more common; we did not invent them. For many years now, prominent atheists such as Arthur Schopenhauer, Carl Sagan, Ann Druyan, Christopher Hitchens, and Sam Harris have made the case that spirituality is important for *everyone*.[2] Fortunately, many writers and leaders on the religious side are now using similarly broad definitions of these terms as well.

Reanimating our Connection to the Sacred

In these pages, we examine traditional Western religious beliefs in the light of current science, and propose viable ways to transform our ancient religious frameworks into new, more open-ended definitions of the sacred—definitions that better fit with reality and also help integrate our sense of ultimate meaning and purpose with the wonder of the cosmos.

What if modern science can help give us an understanding of life and the sacred that is deeper and richer than the one based solely on our ancient traditions? And what if our ancient traditions have insights that transcend time?

Part One: Creation: What We Now Know

It is time to reanimate our connection to the sacred—time to integrate the deepest wisdom of our ancient faiths with scientific knowledge and welcome the different kinds of expertise that each brings to the table. It is time for dialogue that decreases dogmatism and increases humility.

Science and religion ask remarkably similar questions. Combined, they can help us probe the deepest riddles of our existence and address the pressing problems of our times. Combined, they give us an opportunity to rethink religion, reframe spiritual practice, and rediscover a shared sense of purpose. Out of these new connections arises a deeper sense of transcendence—that dimension that lifts us above our singular, isolated selves and connects us with what some might call God, and others the Infinite, the Sacred, or simply Wonder.

Our Ever-Changing Perceptions About God and Reality

After all, our understanding of God and of reality has continually changed through the ages, depending on the scientific knowledge and culture of the times. This is a good thing. If our understanding hadn't changed, we'd still be burning people at the stake for having the gall to claim that the earth is not the center of the universe, with the sun, moon, and stars circling around it—which was taught by the church from the second century CE and upheld by the Christian world for 1,400 years.

The late American mythologist Joseph Campbell pointed out that the religion-versus-science wars of our era are not really fought between religion and science, but rather between two versions of science: ancient concepts of the natural world versus current scientific knowledge. Taking biblical stories about creation literally, as if they were simply old newspaper clippings recounting long-ago events, causes us to miss the larger questions of meaning and mystery that these stories were originally created to address.

More of us are beginning to realize that *all* of reality has elements of the sacred, and that current scientific understanding is a compelling way of helping us to grasp it. We will also incorporate a celebration of change as a key part of these narratives. Rather than something fixed, our cosmic history is a parade of one change after another, and our scientific understanding builds and becomes more nuanced with each new discovery.

Join Us

So please join us as we dive fearlessly and honestly into the ultimate questions: What can we know; how can science illuminate as well as challenge our pictures of the divine; what are the moral repercussions of different beliefs; and what does all of this mean for ourselves, our communities, and our world?

We'd like to update the ancient wisdom of the holy books with the grand and meaningful creation story that we now know to be true. It is a story that encompasses everything from the birth of our universe 13.8 billion years ago, up through the latest revelations of quantum physics and cellular biology—a saga that embraces the challenges and joys of our existence, the values that orient us, and our stumbling attempts to live up to our deepest ideals. A story that inspires us to participate with knowledge *and* wisdom, so that all creation can thrive.

On the one hand, we wrote this book for those of you who have grown disillusioned with a world-denying religion, who are troubled by archaic and hurtful morality and by equally archaic views of science and creation that seem to defy common sense. We'd like to help you unite the best of your religion's ideals, stories, and connections to the sacred, without requiring you to deny the evident truths of science, ethics, and nature.

On the other hand, we wrote this book for those of you who may have grown dissatisfied with forms of atheism that seemed to leave no place for spirituality, values, or a sense of the sacred. In this book we explore ideas about the ultimate that can still speak to the quest for meaning, transcendence, and spiritual fulfillment. We hope to open up a concept of the ultimate that enhances your motivation for branching out, flourishing, and making the world a better place. We will propose ways to do this that don't require people to adhere blindly to yet another fixed worldview, to a system that remains unchanged even when new discoveries come to light.

In short, we have in mind readers across the entire continuum: from those who continue to use the word "God," to agnostics who are unsure, and to those who embrace a humanism without the *G*-word. We'll even play with the idea of using "god" in lowercase for those who find themselves somewhere in the middle. This book is intended for all of us, wherever we are currently traveling on this path called life. Together we can find a way to navigate and celebrate the vitality, mystery, terror, and beauty of this magnificent cosmos, and a way to conceive of our being in the midst of everything that exists. It is our hope that readers, regardless of their belief

Part One: Creation: What We Now Know

systems, will find it a valuable tool for addressing their own burning questions, so they can experience more spiritual understanding, wisdom, and peace in their lives and a greater feeling of kinship with the rest of humanity and the world that sustains us. So let us begin . . . at the beginning.

2

In the Beginning...

IN THE BEGINNING THERE were clashing creation stories. In fact, the history of conflicting creation accounts dates to prehistoric times. As the late noted biologist Edward O. Wilson explained in his book *The Social Conquest of Earth*:

> Since Paleolithic times, each tribe—of which there have been countless thousands—invented its own creation myth... The creation stories gave the members of each tribe an explanation for their existence. It made them feel loved and protected above all other tribes. In return, their gods demanded absolute belief and obedience. And rightly so. The creation myth was the essential bond that held the tribe together. It provided its believers with a unique identity, commanded their fidelity, strengthened order, vouchsafed law, encouraged valor and sacrifice, and offered meaning to the cycles of life and death. No tribe could long survive without the meaning of its existence defined by a creation story. The [only other] option was to weaken, dissolve, and die. In the early history of each tribe, the myth therefore had to be set in stone.[3]

More than three-quarters of people in the Western world adhere, at least nominally, to one of the monotheistic religions that trace a common origin to the biblical accounts in Genesis. For many centuries, the creation stories recounted in Genesis 1 and 2 *were* set in stone. They were our origin stories and the explanation for our existence. Because of modern discoveries, however, today many thinking people dismiss those stories as Bronze Age myths, believing they have nothing left to offer other than historical interest. That ignores the reality that we are still struggling with the questions that the writers of Genesis were originally trying to answer. So it seems appropriate to use those ancient creation accounts as a springboard into the discussion of what insights current science may offer on the issues those stories were created to address.

The Contrasting Genesis Creation Stories

Hebrew scholars have long known that the two creation stories in Genesis were written by authors from two different traditions, each with unique characteristics. One was the Priestly tradition, which uses the generic Hebrew word for God (Elohim); the other was the more conservative Yahwist tradition, which uses God's personal name, Yahweh.

Genesis 1:1—2:3 recounts the priestly tradition's version of creation: God creates everything over a six-day period, with humans as the culmination, and with male and female equally reflecting the glory of God. Genesis 1:27-28 (NLT) sums it up as follows:

> So God created humans in his own image. In the image of God he created them; male and female he created them. Then God blessed them and said, "Be fruitful and multiply. Fill the earth and govern it."

Genesis 2:4-25 recounts the Yahwist tradition's very different version. This one sets up a clear patriarchy: God creates part of the world, and then creates Adam out of dust, only then creating animals, also out of dust, and bringing them to Adam. When God determines that none of the animals are adequate companions for Adam, God creates Eve from one of Adam's ribs as a "helpmate."

Clearly these ancient writers were addressing the same questions we wonder about today:

Why am I here?
What is my place in the universe?
Why are we the way that we are?
What about the differences between men and women?
Is there a purpose to life?

They were also attempting to explain the earth's incredible diversity, something we understand much better today.

In the Beginning . . .

Since both the priestly and Yahwist traditions were popular, the scholars who transcribed the sacred Jewish stories that would become Genesis used both of their accounts. Eventually many believers would come to assume that the stories were fully consistent. (They are not.)

Subsequent biblical creation debates centered on whether these biblical creation texts should be taken allegorically or literally. That also began fairly early on. In the first century CE, the prominent Jewish scholar Philo of Alexandria argued that it would be a mistake to think creation actually happened in six days. And in the early fifth century CE, Saint Augustine, one of the Christian church's most influential theologians, wrote that biblical texts, including the creation accounts, should be taken allegorically rather than literally when they contradict what we know from science and reason. After all, he pointed out, as our reason is a gift from God, we should use it.

What We Now Know

The details of how creation actually took place have major and exciting things to say about our nature and that of the universe. They help us answer questions about how we came to be and why we are the way we are far more convincingly than the creation stories of the ancients, which were limited to what people were able to observe and imagine thousands of years ago.

The scientific study of the origins of life, humanity, and the universe only came into its own in recent history. Those of us who are interested in questions of ultimate origins—whether we believe in a God or not—are fortunate to have been born in this era.

Evolution first began to be widely understood in the mid-1800s and early 1900s. It has come a long way since then, especially since the late 1980s, when automated methods of DNA sequencing were introduced, enabling scientists to track species' genetic inheritance.

Other crucial pieces of the puzzle are being supplied by systems biology, sociocultural studies of evolution, evolutionary psychology, and neuroscience, disciplines that are still in their scientific infancy. These are supplying massive amounts of new data about humanity's progression from a tribal world to the Information Age.

Think about how far we have come. As recently as the 1950s, there were only primitive calculating machines; computers didn't even exist. Now most of us carry unbelievably sophisticated computers in our hip pockets in the form of smartphones.

Part One: Creation: What We Now Know

We now understand far more about our common kinship as offshoots of the one tree of evolution and the effects of the rapid changes brought about by technology. Further, we understand the evolutionary and biological reasons for our instinctive responses and learned behaviors—both positive and negative.

Quantum physics (the physics of the extremely minuscule particles and fundamental forces that make up the basic building blocks of the universe) was only beginning to be explored in the late 1800s, and didn't really begin to develop until the 1920s. Equally, modern astrophysics (the study of what's beyond our solar system, including distant planets, stars, galaxies, supernovas, and black holes) and modern cosmology (the study of the origin and eventual fate of the universe) only took off with the initial hypothesis of the Big Bang in 1931. Since then, breakthroughs in space navigation in the 1960s have made it possible to launch satellites to capture pictures and data from space beyond the reach of Earth-based telescopes, and increasingly powerful supercomputers have been developed to process that information. Now, the discoveries are multiplying exponentially.

We are fortunate to be living in an era when the miracle of the creation of our particular universe is no longer a matter of mythological conjecture, but a verifiable history, written in the cosmos. Let us begin, once again, to recount that supreme miracle, our Genesis, not in ancient Hebrew, Greek, or Arabic, but in the universal language of science.

In the beginning there was the Big Bang ...

3

We Are All Star-Stuff

So . . . here we are, careening through space on this tiny spinning planet where we make our home. We live in the somewhat shabby outer suburbs of a nondescript galaxy, one of hundreds of billions of other galaxies in the universe. All that protects us from the frigid cosmic void is a thin blanket of air, held to Earth's surface by gravity.

As we circle our Sun at 66,700 miles per hour, our modest little solar system is also zooming around the center of our galaxy, the Milky Way, at 514,500 miles per hour. The Milky Way, in turn (which, besides our solar system, contains more than 100 billion stars, many with their own retinues of planets), is moving at about 1.3 million miles per hour with respect to the universe itself (measured by its speed relative to the cosmic microwave background radiation left over from the Big Bang).

At 100,000 light-years across (1 light-year = 5.9 trillion miles), our galaxy is a runt compared with more robust galaxies such as Hercules A, which measures 1.5 million light-years across. Hercules A and the other 100 billion to 200 billion galaxies in the universe are also speeding along at extremely high velocities, most of them moving away from us.

As it happens, however, our nearest galactic neighbor, the Andromeda Galaxy, is barreling along in our direction and will sideswipe our Milky Way in about 2 billion years. Astrophysicists think the forces involved in the collision might gradually push our Sun out farther from the central black holes of both galaxies, so if our descendants have managed to survive in other places than our planet, they may even be able to watch the show, including the resulting changes in our night sky's constellations.

Is the End of the World the End of Us?

About seven billion years from now, however, our star, the sun, will enter its last stage of life, becoming a red giant—an expanding, dying star—and consuming Mercury, Venus, and possibly Earth, or at the very least, burning off all our atmosphere and water. If our descendants haven't colonized other parts of space by then, humanity will be toast. Fortunately, seven billion years is plenty of advance warning.

At this point we leave the real, outward observations of pure physical science and enter the inner ones of metaphysics, that is, of philosophical and spiritual conjecture. Say our plans go awry and humanity dies.

We will hold a more extensive discussion of afterlife concepts later, in Chapter 10. The question here is, What, if anything, has afterlife potential, based on what we now know about reality?

In spite of our minuscule size as humans, and our seemingly inconsequential place in the unimaginable vastness of the universe, it is actually not unreasonable to view our consciousness as remarkable and to wonder whether it might continue in some way after our bodies are gone. That's because we happen to be the most complex entity that scientists know about, so far. In fact, most of Earth's life is more complex than a star, even mosquitoes.

Lord Martin Rees, professor of cosmology and astrophysics at the University of Cambridge, has said, "A star is a huge ball of gas, and is so hot that all chemicals are broken down into their atomic constituencies. There's no complex structure. Whereas even a small insect has layer upon layer of structure—protein, cells, and all the rest of it."[4]

Humans are, of course, a huge leap in complexity over bugs. In fact, each of us is a highly conscious portal to the universe. Therefore, it is fair to ask, "Is the universe (or a mind behind the universe) using us to understand itself?" Is it using us, who are made of star-stuff, to contemplate its stars? What about us might be a hint of the deeper nature of the universe? It is truly a mind-blowing thought. It brings us back to the long-debated question of whether we and our earthly cohabitants were spawned by the Big Bang through a random series of events, or whether there was some kind of divine purpose behind the events that caused us to emerge.

To begin to address this question, it will help to back up at this point and give a brief history of cosmology.

A Brief History of Cosmology

According to the Greek philosopher Aristotle (384–322 BCE), the universe, including Earth, was eternal. It always was and always would be.

In the Middle Ages, however, philosophers in the Jewish, Muslim, and Christian traditions pointed out that this view created problems for the biblical account of a God who created everything out of nothing in the beginning. So, the church's bishop of Paris, Étienne Tempier, banned the teaching along with numerous other Aristotelian doctrines in his *Condemnation of 1270*, and religious philosophers began seeking evidence and logical arguments that would support the idea that the universe had a finite past. They were part of a long tradition of people of faith who were involved in cosmological investigations and speculations.

By the late fourteenth century, after plagues and famines had decimated nearly half the European population, and conflicts, including armed revolts, raged in the church, the idea of direct empirical study of the earth and the heavens was reborn. After all, hadn't God established a creation governed by predictable natural laws? Shouldn't humans be able to study the natural world, in order to discover and understand those underlying laws? And humans began again to do just that.

As our measurable and experimentally verified knowledge grew, our desire for more knowledge that could be based on reason and observation grew with it—and so, more and more, human intellectual powers were focused on the natural world.

It lay in the very nature of the scientific quest to let truth be dictated by observation and reason and not by the political, religious, or academic establishment. The early scientists insisted that we should affirm only those theories that are consistent with the data, the theories that best explain or predict what our observations and experiments show us.

In his play about the life of Galileo, Bertolt Brecht captures this central drive of science. We see the great astronomer being condemned by the papal authorities for teaching that the earth moves around the sun, rather than being the stationary center of the universe. The authorities leave and the lights dim. Then Galileo lifts his fist and yells after them, "*But it moves*

Part One: Creation: What We Now Know

nonetheless!" If that's what the most rigorous science shows, no authority can change it; no papal proclamation can make it otherwise.

Because the religious establishment dismissed scientific results that seemed to conflict with the Bible and traditional church teachings, early modern science gradually insisted on complete independence from the church. A mutual mistrust grew up between church hierarchies and leading scientists—even when those scientists were members of the clergy.

This mistrust increased in the 1800s after Darwin suggested that evidence pointed to the conclusion that natural processes, rather than divine decree, had produced the world's species, and that therefore God might not be necessary for explaining the presence of man and woman among the animals. These claims hit religious authorities even closer to home than talk of planets and stars. After all, it had been a basic assumption in the biblical traditions that each species was eternal and unchanging, and that man and woman had been directly created by the hand of God. The question was famously debated at Oxford in 1860, where the Christian scholar Bishop Samuel Wilberforce countered the arguments of the Darwinist scientist Thomas Huxley by asking him whether he was descended from monkeys on his grandfather's or his grandmother's side.

Every now and again, however, a major scientific breakthrough would cause people of faith to wonder whether the findings of science could actually strengthen the idea that God created the universe. The Big Bang was one of them.

By the early 1900s, astronomers began noticing that light from distant galaxies was shifted more toward the red end of the light spectrum and began to ask why. That phenomenon, called redshift, happens when light from a faraway star or galaxy increases in wavelength because it is moving away from us. (Blueshift occurs when the object moves closer to us and the wavelengths become shorter, shifting toward the blue end of the light spectrum.)

Stargazers who observed this redshift, including the Belgian Catholic priest and scientist Georges Lemaître, began suggesting that the universe might actually be expanding—contradicting the previously accepted model of a fixed-size universe. Lemaître took the debate a step further when he proposed his "Hypothesis of the Primeval Atom," published by London's Royal Astronomical Society in 1931. In this famous paper, he concluded that the universe was not eternal after all; instead, it must have originated, with a sudden explosion as its point of origin.

Initially Lemaître's proposal was quite controversial. In fact, "Big Bang" was a term invented by Fred Hoyle, one of his detractors, intended as a sarcastic put-down of Lemaître's hypothesis. But in 1965, Arno Penzias and Robert Wilson were able to measure the temperature of the microwave background radiation present in the universe. Physicists such as Robert Dicke quickly began to investigate, and concluded that this background radiation must be left over from an initial explosion and subsequent expansion of the universe. A great deal of other evidence was found that gave strong credence to the idea that the universe had a point of origin. The Big Bang theory became widely accepted, and its colorful label stuck.

The Creation Point

We now know that our particular universe originated about 13.8 billion years ago, most likely from a "singularity," a point of unimaginable mass density. Since the laws of physics break down at a singularity, scientists can't know for sure what happened, but the most plausible and widely accepted hypothesis is that the universe arose out of fluctuations in the quantum vacuum.

We've all been taught that a vacuum contains nothing—not even air molecules. But that's not true at the quantum level. At the quantum level, energy fluctuations are constantly occurring. Charged particles are continually forming in the quantum field and then disappearing again in fractions of a nanosecond. The singularity that created our universe was an exception. By some quirk it didn't disappear; it took off. What happened before the Big Bang is still a matter of debate among cosmologists, but we now know a tremendous amount about what happened after it—beginning with the very first microseconds of existence.

In the instants immediately after the Big Bang, the universe was unbelievably hot (about 100 million-trillion-trillion degrees), and extremely dense. As it expanded and cooled, the first particles—quarks and electrons—began appearing. A few millionths of a second later, the quarks began aggregating to produce protons and neutrons. The incredibly rapid expansion caused the universe to balloon in size from a point smaller than an atom to something the size of a golf ball (100 trillion-trillion times larger than its subatomic beginning size) in less than a second. This "cosmic inflation" was so powerful that it made wrinkles in our initial space-time continuum and set off distinctive gravitational wave patterns.

Part One: Creation: What We Now Know

Within the first three minutes after the Big Bang, the incandescent colliding protons, neutrons, and electrons began combining to make hydrogen, helium, and eventually trace amounts of lithium. The first elements had emerged. (If you are rusty on your high school chemistry, hydrogen, helium, and lithium are, respectively, elements 1, 2, and 3 on the periodic table: the simplest and lightest of the elements, ranked by the number of protons in their nucleus.)

The cosmos continued to rapidly expand and cool, and, to make a long, long story incredibly short, about 400 million years later, it had formed elemental gasses. These gasses then formed into clumps, which began collapsing through gravitational pull to form the first stars and galaxies. These, in turn, blazed out energy that burned up much of the widespread hydrogen in the universe. After using up most of their fuel, the bigger stars collapsed in on themselves and then exploded into supernovas, bodies one billion times as brilliant as our sun. The supernovas generated even more elements, up through uranium (element 92). Just to give you an example of the power of supernovas, humans can produce enough heat to form even a relatively simple element like iron (element 26) only by using a thermonuclear reactor.

Let There Be Carbon

Among the elements produced by the supernovas' thermonuclear power was carbon (element 6). In several more billion years, this simple element would become the basic building block of life on Earth, because it is ideally structured to connect with a multitude of other molecules.

While the elements were being formed, the same processes were generating the galaxies, the second-generation stars, and their planets. Finally, about nine billion years after the Big Bang, our own Sun and solar system begin to emerge.

How do we know all this? By combining astronomical observations and measurements with knowledge from particle physics, cosmologists can reconstruct the various stages of our cosmic evolution with great precision. For example, based on their research, in 1948 Ralph Alpher and other scientists predicted the existence of cosmic microwave background radiation (CMB) left over from the Big Bang. In 1965, scientists in a Bell Telephone lab who were building a high-powered radio receiver picked up radiation that was acting as a source of excess noise, and realized with excitement that it must be actual CMB. Later, the Wilkinson Microwave Anisotropy Probe (WMAP) satellite, which launched in 2001, began providing amazing images of the cosmic microwave background radiation as it existed a short while after the Big Bang: pictures of the universe when it was less than 400,000 years old!

How were these images possible? Radiation travels at the speed of light (about 671 million miles per hour). Whenever we are looking at stars and galaxies, we are seeing them as they were in the distant past, because their light has traveled so long to get to us. Most of the stars we can see with the naked eye are 10 to 100 light-years away, which means we see them as they were 10 to 100 years ago. When stargazers use a telescope to observe our neighboring Andromeda galaxy, they are seeing it as it was about 2.5 million years ago.

Since the first primitive space telescopes were launched in the mid to late 1960s, the technology has grown by leaps and bounds. Today a routine Wikipedia list of space telescopes grouped by the major frequency ranges they cover includes gamma ray, X-ray, ultraviolet, visible, infrared, microwave, and radio; there are also space telescopes that collect particles and electrons, as well as instruments to detect gravitational waves.[5]

That *excludes* all missions with specific targets in our solar system, as well as observation satellites for missions targeting Earth, which are completely separate categories.

The most famous and successful space telescope, the Hubble, launched into low-Earth orbit in 1990, was specifically designed to be maintained in space by astronauts. Since that time, five shuttle missions have repaired, upgraded, and replaced systems on the telescope, and many of its observations have led to breakthroughs in astrophysics, including nailing down the rate of expansion of the universe.

Most recently, the James Webb Infrared Space Telescope, launched on Christmas Day 2021, has given us the most exciting "baby pictures" we've seen yet of our universe just after the Big Bang. A number of the Webb observations are raising serious questions about the standard account we've just given. To name just one example, relatively large black holes existed sooner after the Big Bang than the standard model predicts. So stay tuned for more exciting developments!

Part One: Creation: What We Now Know

Why Major Discoveries Come So Much Faster Now

These new data and the theories they confirm provide a snapshot of how rapidly science is now moving. In 240 BCE, the Greco-Egyptian astronomer Eratosthenes used his observations of the sun's movement to calculate that the earth was a sphere, even estimating its circumference to within one percent of its actual value. At the time, most people thought he was crazy—wasn't it obvious that the world was flat?

It wasn't until 1,760 years later that Ferdinand Magellan's voyage around the world (1519–22) gave observational proof that the earth was round. And Magellan had to keep his itinerary secret from his crew, or they would have refused to come with him, for fear of falling off the edge of the earth.

It took much less time (just 450 years) for us to gain the next proof of the earth's spherical shape: the beloved and famous photo taken by the Apollo 17 crew in 1972, showing the "blue marble" floating in space. Because of the knowledge and technology now at our disposal, major discoveries and verifications are coming much faster. In fact, the pace is increasing exponentially.

The Metaphysics of the Big Bang . . .

But back to creation: Although the Big Bang could have happened without a Divine Creator, it certainly allows for the possibility of one. By the 1950s, the theologically loaded theory had begun to capture the popular imagination, and in 1951 the Catholic Church officially pronounced the Big Bang to be in agreement with the Bible. Many religious believers began celebrating the Big Bang as actual evidence of the creation of the universe by God.

In truth, however, the Big Bang neither proves nor disproves the existence of God. After all, the concept of a preexisting divine being setting the Big Bang in motion is just as mind-boggling and incredible to contemplate as the idea of a preexisting quantum vacuum suddenly inflating. Where in the world did *either one* come from? Or, as the philosopher Gottfried Leibniz memorably put the question: Why is there something rather than nothing?

When you add the "fine-tuning argument" to the Big Bang, however, God becomes more believable, even if we can't explain why or how God exists. The fine-tuning argument asks, "What are the odds that the universe would produce our particular kind of life?" It turns out that the odds are astronomically against us. So many of the laws of physics, the physical constants, and other conditions have to be within an extremely narrow range for the universe itself to exist at all: the narrow span of values that allow the stable atoms and molecules to form matter as we know it, the mass of the universe, the rate of its expansion—you can go on and on. If each of these constants did not have almost exactly the value it now has, you would not have the conditions for our kind of life. There's only one chance in billions that all these factors would come together on their own in exactly this way. Hence, fine-tuning advocates argue, it is highly likely that a being with intelligence and purpose was involved in setting up this exact set of conditions. Score one for God.

Except that the Argument Works Only if There Is Just One Universe

What if there is more than one? A number of physicists are now telling us that those same equations that explain the Big Bang also suggest that there should be many other universes. A "multiverse," although still not proven, might be a setback for the fine-tuners, and forfeit the point we just awarded to God.

Remember how, in describing the creation point, we noted that quantum fluctuations in the vacuum of space are going on all the time? The odds of a fluctuation lasting long enough to create another singularity, resulting in another Big Bang and a new universe, seem extremely minuscule. But over vast amounts of time, the equations say, it will likely happen again, and again—so there will always be other universes, and new cycles of time to mark their progress.

"Multiverse" describes the sum total of all those universes. According to this hypothesis, the multiverse contains an *infinite* number of universes that each have their own fundamental constants. They range from universes completely different from ours, to universes that could conceivably be almost identical. A quantum vacuum could fluctuate in exactly the same way as the singularity that produced our cosmos, and create a world and history exactly like ours except that Taylor in the front row of your college physics class is wearing a green shirt and not a blue one today. That is theoretically possible, given infinite time. Meanwhile, there will be other universes with completely different kinds of life, based on a completely different set of constants.

If there are infinitely many universes, and we happen to inhabit one capable of producing life, does that prove God exists? No, say the multiverse theorists—obviously, it was just a matter of chance that *our particular universe* would be hospitable to life.

Imagine that infinitely many universes, all with different characteristics, were and are bubbling and exploding into existence in this cosmic sea of infinite, eternal inflation. Isn't it clear that it was only a matter of time before a space-time bubble with our universe's particular constants would pop up? In other words, sooner or later *some* universe would hit the conscious-life jackpot, and ours was the one. In fact, if there are infinitely many universes, it is probable that billions and billions of them contain life. Remember, it is only in a "winning universe" that there are observers who can stop to ask the question, "Why am I here?"

If the multiverse theory is true, the fine-tuning argument isn't nearly as convincing. In that case, we're back to a modified version of the conundrum we already encountered: The concept of a preexisting Being creating a cosmic multiverse is at least as incredible and mind-boggling to contemplate as a cosmic multiverse creating our universe. Again, where in the world did either one—Being or multiverse—come from?

Of course, postulating an infinite number of other universes is not without its own problems. After all, where the heck are these multiple universes? If we can't ever access or observe them, what scientific grounds can there be for postulating their existence? For a theory to be part of physics, it needs data and laws that we can test, but how can we observe or do experiments on universes that are currently (and perhaps forever) beyond our reach? It looks as if we're getting back into philosophy and mysticism. Which just shows how challenging and constantly changing is the line between physics and metaphysics.

The debate continues. Numerous prominent physicists, including the late Stephen Hawking, have concluded that the equations of Big Bang cosmology *require* infinite universes. Someday, they argue (a someday that right now is only imaginable in science fiction), descendants of humans may find a way to move beyond our three dimensions to access one of the other universes, if they do indeed exist.

That idea seems extremely far-fetched; but think back to ancient times, when *everything* was metaphysics. A plethora of gods caused the sun to rise and set, the rain to fall, the plants to grow, the rivers to flow, and so on. Humans invented all kinds of rituals they thought would keep each of the gods happy, so that their crops would grow and their hunts would succeed.

From Metaphysics to Testable Facts

As science and technology progressed, however, it became clear that, for example, good irrigation, fertilization, and pest control were much more likely to guarantee successful harvests than the sacrifice of an animal to a particular harvest god.

The more we learn, it seems, the more explanations shift over to the side of science. Today's metaphysical speculation may be replaced by tomorrow's testable fact.

Back in the early 1970s, Joel Primack (known as the smartest guy in the room) at the University of California, Santa Cruz made some predictions about the properties of quarks. He used mathematical equations and minimal experimental data. Later he got a call from the Stanford Linear Accelerator, SLAC, asking him to come up for a presentation. As he sat in the audience, the scientists at SLAC publicly announced that their most recent experiments had just confirmed Primack's predictions about quarks in real time; the quantum world had shown itself to be exactly as Primack's purely mathematical calculations had led him to believe it. Primack, an atheist, once said that this was the closest to a religious experience he had ever had. We would describe such experiences as sacred—as we said before, it is time to expand the definition of "sacred" to include "secular" experiences as well.

The God Particle

Earlier, in 1964, physicist Peter Higgs proposed the existence of what became known as the Higgs boson—the subatomic particle that caused the energy sources produced by the Big Bang to have mass. It was a crucial building block for the universe—and for the equations that describe it. Higgs's brilliant mathematical speculations led him to calculations that set the stage for one of the most sophisticated and stunning scientific verifications in the history of physics.

If you have followed with any enthusiasm the great discoveries of science in our time, this one should have grabbed your attention. If scientists succeeded in detecting signs of the Higgs field, they would be standing on the threshold of brilliant new discoveries about the fundamentals of physics.

For almost fifty years experimental physicists had been working to detect this particle, one of the most elusive ever sought. Finally, in 2012, two teams working independently at the world's most powerful accelerator,

Part One: Creation: What We Now Know

CERN's Large Hadron Collider in Switzerland, were able to detect not only its existence but also most of the qualities that Professor Higgs (and others) had predicted back in 1964.

The confirmation of this crucial scientific discovery did, however, remind us once again of the ultimate metaphysical question. Why *are* we here? Why *is* there something rather than nothing?

Science and the Sacred: Sharing the Wonder

Religion and science are not normally viewed as complementary, to put it mildly—but why should they not be? Remember that ever-moving line between physics and metaphysics? In his 1994 book, *Pale Blue Dot*, astrophysicist Carl Sagan wrote:

> How is it that hardly any major religion has looked at science and concluded, 'This is better than we thought! The universe is much bigger than our prophets said, grander, more subtle, more elegant'? Instead, they say, 'No, no, no! My god is a little god, and I want him to stay that way.' A religion, old or new, that stressed the magnificence of the universe as revealed by modern science might be able to draw forth reserves of reverence and awe hardly tapped by the conventional faiths.[6]

Things have improved since Sagan wrote those words. Contrary to the stereotype of belief as anti-science, an increasing number of people of faith are finding that their religions are quite compatible with astrophysics as well as cosmology. Buddhists, Hindus, Taoists, Christians, Jews, and Muslims have all written on the commonalities between physics and their core religious and spiritual ideas, especially in the more mystical and spiritual strands of each of these faiths. And their picture of the divine is much deeper and more unfathomable than the God described by their fundamentalist colleagues.

Cosmology and Astrophysics
An Existential Summary of Chapter 3

WE PAUSE HERE TO summarize what insight the above concepts of astrophysics and cosmology might give us into the questions of our existence:

- Our universe is extremely inhospitable to life; it has been around for some 13.8 billion years; and we (modern humans) only emerged about 120,000 years ago. So, you'd be hard pressed to argue that an omnipotent God set everything up for our benefit, especially since natural processes, rather than divine decree, produced Earth's species, including ourselves. We look more like a brief afterthought or accident in the great scheme of creation.

On the other hand, certain cosmic characteristics have spiritually promising possibilities:

- Interconnectedness is fundamental to the universe.
- The universe is composed of unimaginable quantities of mass and energy, of which we are small portions. Humans, and all other things in our universe, are related to one another as specific forms that this incredible flow of energy has taken. Truly, we are all star-stuff.
- We are also, along with all of creation, co-creators of our own present and future, which are ever-changing.
- We are the most complex entity that scientists know about, and far more complex than stars and galaxies. Our consciousness is so unique

and remarkable that it is not too far-fetched to wonder whether it will continue in some way after our bodies are gone.

- There is immense beauty in our universe, which we experience through our senses. The mathematics in which the fundamental physical laws are expressed is equally beautiful, staggering in its simplicity and elegance. Most of us, no matter what we believe, feel a sense of awe and humility when confronted with this beauty, whether we see it in nature, the heavens, a cathedral, music, or a piece of art.

- We end this chapter, and introduce the next, with a delightful quote from evolutionary cosmologist Brian Swimme, describing a spirituality that encompasses *everything* in the universe, both as a whole and in its parts:

> You take hydrogen gas, you leave it alone, and it turns into rose bushes, giraffes, and humans. That's the short version. The reason I like that version is that hydrogen gas is odorless and colorless, and in the prejudice of our Western civilization, we see it as just material stuff. There's not much there... The point is that if humans are spiritual, then hydrogen's spiritual. It is an incredible opportunity to escape the traditional dualism—you know, spirit is up there; matter is down here. Actually, it is different. You have matter all the way through, and so you have spirit all the way through. So that's why I love the short version.[7]

4

The Dynamic Drive at Life's Core

IN ORDER TO EXAMINE what the natural world might tell us about God, we need to look at the process that forms and undergirds all of life on Earth: evolution. In explaining the development of all of the species, the theory of evolution has helped us map the history of our own. This means that it replaces some of the myths about human origin that have satisfied us for thousands of years. Some people find this exciting and fascinating; others find it deeply troubling.

Millions of believers from all religions have taken the time to investigate the biological processes of evolution, and have accepted them as facts without losing their faith. In fact, for the first time in history, ever, evolution is now accepted by a majority of Americans. In an article published August 20, 2021, the University of Michigan put the number at 54 percent—just a decade after a statistical dead heat between those who accepted evolution and those who didn't.

A growing number of religious and spiritual thinkers point out that evolution offers a far richer picture of creation than the various scriptures' more static supernatural explanations. Understanding the creative process of evolution can deepen the sense of significance, awe, and reverence in our lives, whether we believe God was involved or not.

There are, however, still a significant number of holdouts who believe it is impossible to hold on to your faith and still accept the facts of evolution. We look at this group in Appendix A to illuminate the contrasts between two very different claims: a creation that happened through natural processes over time, versus one created by an omnipotent God.

Here, we describe the facts:

Evolution 101

Evolution is the dynamic drive at the core of life. Nothing makes sense in biology without it: neither the cosmic record, the geological record, the fossil record, nor the genealogy our DNA traces along the ever-branching tree of life. A sense of how evolution works is crucial for grasping our era's breakthroughs in medicine, disease control, forensic science, crop hybridization, neurobiology, and a myriad of other disciplines.

The Hebrew sages who wrote the Genesis accounts, like the authors of other world religions' ancient sacred texts, composed creation stories based on the knowledge, beliefs, and worldviews of their time. They could not have supposed that God favored the gradual and chaotic emergence of species produced by evolution, because they had no means of observing or deducing such a long and slow process. The animals and plants they knew remained the same from generation to generation. Therefore, it was logical to think that God created them all at once, intending them to be companions and sustenance for humans.

When we cling to these ancient stories literally, rather than learning to interpret them metaphorically, we diminish the richness of the lessons they have to teach us. We also create needless stumbling blocks to accepting and expanding the awe-inspiring truths that science has to offer.

Contrary to the literalist interpretations of Genesis, the fact is that modern science, the structure of our DNA, and the fossil records show that we are not only related to apes; we are also related to algae . . . and to every other living thing, down to the first single-celled organisms. Does accepting this primitive lineage mean that we must reject the possibility of divine creativity? Not at all.

If, as believers often proclaim, God is the God of all truth, then why would God consider them more devout for believing an account of life's origins that has been proven empirically false? In fact, if we humans had known earlier in our history that we were directly and genetically related to every other species, perhaps we would have treated our fellow creations with more reverence and care.

We might also have understood sooner why we tend to behave the way we do. Our biological lineage heavily influenced our destiny for thousands of years and continues to do so. Our large brains gradually produced culture and language, which became crucial factors influencing the evolution of our species. Today, ever more frequent breakthroughs in technology are enabling us to modify our environment and even our biological blueprint and thus co-create our future evolution in brand-new ways.

We will explore these amazing (and scary) new capabilities later. But first, let's pause to examine how, exactly, the earlier branches on the tree of life eventually produced the small branch that led to us, and what that might suggest about the fundamental questions of our existence.

The Basics

The fundamentals of biological evolution are not hard to grasp. They can be summarized in as few as three words: *descent with modifications*. Here's how it works.

Evolution relies on there being different gene frequencies in a population. These genes affect the population's physical characteristics. The characteristics most important for evolution are those that enable the organism to survive long enough to reproduce. Survival advantages may include better ability to find food, better ways to avoid predators, better ways to resist disease, having legions of offspring, and so on. If the members of a particular species do not survive long enough to reproduce, that species will become extinct.

If a new combination of genes from the parents (in the case of sexual reproduction) or a new mutation (in the case of both sexual and asexual reproduction) results in new characteristics that give the offspring or clones a survival advantage that makes them better adapted to their environment, those individuals are more likely to survive and reproduce, and their genes are more likely to be passed on to the next generation.

This process is how evolution works and is called natural selection, popularly known as survival of the fittest. The offspring most suited to their environment not only survive and reproduce and come to dominate the species, but over time will gradually evolve new advantages, as additional new gene combinations and mutations give them even more favorable characteristics.

Part One: Creation: What We Now Know

This goes two ways, of course: Disadvantageous mutations can persist when they don't cause immediate extinction. For example, having the sickle-cell trait provides significant protection from malaria, so that genetic mutation has persisted in areas where malaria is prevalent, even though parents who both have the trait are more likely to produce a child with sickle-cell anemia, a terrible disease. There are also many mutations that have little to no apparent value, positive or negative, yet they persist across existing species.

The blueprint inside the genes that allows organisms to make copies of themselves is an amazing molecule that evolved to hold all the bits of an individual's genetic information: deoxyribonucleic acid, or DNA.

DNA explains why reproduction in nature can be either sexual or asexual. Single-celled organisms, such as protozoa and bacteria, generally reproduce asexually. They simply divide in two, essentially cloning themselves. Because their lives are precarious, they tend to divide constantly in order to increase the odds of their descendants' survival. Mutations that occur during the division process get passed along (unless they cause the organism to die before it reproduces).

The offspring from sexual reproduction have more variety than the offspring from asexual reproduction. When sperm and egg unite, the genetic information from two parents is combined in different ways, producing a new individual with many more individual traits than one created by cloning, and with far more potential for evolving new survival traits.

Plants, because they are stationary, originally depended on asexual reproduction mechanisms, which many retain today, producing offspring through spores, roots, bulbs, and tubers. These asexual mechanisms, far more complex than single-cell cloning, have allowed plant species to evolve with proportionately greater variety. But the offspring they produced often grew so close to their parents that an entire colony could be wiped out through a single natural disaster or passing creature. Because of this, many plant species evolved both sexual and asexual reproduction.

Strawberry plants, for example, produce clones of themselves with runners that grow roots as soon as they touch moist soil. They also reproduce sexually when their flowers are fertilized by pollen from other strawberry plants, brought by bees, other insects, or even wind, and develop strawberries—fruits covered with tiny seeds. Passing birds, squirrels, and other critters carry the strawberries away to eat, dispersing the seeds to new areas, where they may grow into new strawberry plants with characteristics from both parent plants—and, possibly, mutations that may or may not give them a new survival advantage.

Most animals—mammals, birds, reptiles, fish, insects, and others—reproduce sexually. But some, like corals, snails, aphids, certain sharks, and certain lizards, can reproduce asexually as well, when there is no mate of their own species around. Virgin Komodo dragons, for example, will lay a clutch of eggs, and some of these unfertilized eggs will be viable and produce baby Komodos. Others will be duds, suitable only for scrambled eggs (assuming you know how to gather them without getting your hand bitten off).

Whether a species' reproduction is asexual or sexual, transmission of the genetic blueprint from parent(s) to offspring is almost perfect. Fortunately, not completely so. If it were, organisms could not evolve, adapting to an ever-changing environment in new and remarkable ways.

Although random mutations of genes produce many novel features in offspring over time, most of these variations are not useful. Some make no immediate visible difference in the offspring's ability to flourish (though they may help the species adapt and survive thousands of generations later, in a different environment). Others are harmful, resulting in offspring that are sterile or less able to flourish, and these variant offspring often die out.

But every now and then, a particular mutation will give the new organism an advantage over others in its environment, and thus a better chance at survival.

Survival of the Most Cooperative

In popular culture, "survival of the fittest" is used more often than "natural selection" to describe this process. Unfortunately, the phrase has been misunderstood, especially in the past, to mean "survival of the mightiest and most aggressive." That is a gross oversimplification and distortion of how evolution actually works.

The fittest organism (i.e., the one that is most successful at producing offspring that survive to reproduce) may sometimes be the mightiest and most aggressive, but it can also be the one that is smartest at anticipating how other species will behave, or one that's quickest at running away, or the predator or prey that is best camouflaged, or the sneakiest male that impregnates the most females, or the female best able to hide her children creatively, or that produces the largest number of eggs. (The female sunfish, for example, can release up to 300 million eggs at one time.) The processes of evolution have resulted in countless survival strategies.

Usually, however, it is *the most cooperative species* that turn out to be the fittest, although cooperation is not a quality that the general public usually associates with evolution. Once you make the connection, however, it is easy to come up with examples: ants, bees, prairie dogs, herding animals, humans . . . even corals and many plants survive by cooperating with beneficial bacteria or fungi that give them vital nutrients.

In primates and early human species, groups of individuals that learned to work together cooperatively had better survival rates than those that didn't—hence the development of tribes. Both monogamous males and males that impregnated many females had evolutionary advantages. Males that mated with one female and shared the care of their mutual offspring were more likely to have offspring that lived to adulthood and reproduced in their turn. A male that impregnated multiple females was unable to help look after all of his offspring, but if he was a member of a tribe, the odds were still good that one or more of his offspring would survive.

Even Our Cells Work Together

Our cells are descended from single-celled organisms that once competed with one another but now work together as a well-connected system. Within our cells, the mitochondria that provide energy are descended from free-living bacteria that gave up their autonomy for a cooperative existence. Our microbial cells outnumber our human cells ten to one. The microbes help us digest our food, develop our immune system, and much more. We couldn't survive without them, nor could they survive without us.

Cooperation is one of the most common survival traits in nature across all species. So it turns out that many of our core religious and secular values—love one another, treat others as you'd like to be treated—make biological sense as well.

Breeding Cauliflower from Cabbage . . .

Often before a new species emerges, there will be an ongoing explosion of variety in all the local species with numerous mutations—some mundane, some exotic, some grotesque. Then nature—the local climate, geographic contours, mineral makeup, flora, and fauna—winnows these new developments down to the forms that work best in that region. In other words, a believer might say, God uses variety as a way to explore biological possibilities and to create the future of the biosphere.

Farmers used evolutionary principles for centuries, long before they understood how genetic traits are passed on. For example, by selecting different characteristics of wild mustard plants that they wanted to accentuate, vegetable breeders obtained cabbage, kale, collard greens, kohlrabi, broccoli, cauliflower, and more, all of which have wild mustard as their common ancestor. Such experimentation has resulted in a wonderful variety of fruits, vegetables, and grains to grace our tables.

... and Mutants from Fruit Flies

The shorter the organism's life cycle, the faster a novelty can emerge. That's why we have so many more species of insects than mammals.

Take common fruit flies—they grow from egg to adult in eight to ten days and lay up to 500 eggs during their two-week lifespan. On San Francisco's Exploratorium website, you'll see a section on mutant fruit flies. By selectively breeding fruit flies with certain mutations, you can get flies with double wings (like dragonflies), short wings, curly wings, black bodies, yellow bodies, weirdly colored eyes, no eyes, and so on.

If you let these mutants loose in nature, most of them disappear rather quickly, since they are less fit for survival than normal fruit flies. But let's say one of the mutations is advantageous in the fruit flies' new environment—perhaps the ones with yellow coloring blend in better with the yellow-hued fruits and plants in a certain area, so that predators are less likely to find the flies and eat them. Then, obviously, more of the yellow fruit flies will survive and reproduce, and over time, more and more of the fruit flies in that area will be yellow.

Evolution Simply Describes How Nature Works

The evidence shows that we, and the rest of living creation, were rather messily and haphazardly formed, beginning with the simplest early organisms and developing into today's vast array of species, in fits and starts over very long periods of time. Inherited changes in some species caused them to have better reproductive success and play a stronger role in the ongoing evolution of life, while other less successful species died out. The fossil, genetic, and geological records have clearly and beautifully recorded this story of the gradual evolution of complex life, right up to humankind. Perhaps, on some distant day, creatures far surpassing us will be learning about their relationship to us in their cells and our fossils.

In fact, it seems to us that the process of evolution fits very well the God of love that the Bible proclaims. In religious terms, you could describe physics and evolution as the world creating itself in response to the call of God. This is a much more playful, fascinating, and benign picture of God than the Young-Earth Creationists' magical God who created everything perfectly in six 24-hour days and then cursed the earth and all its future generations with death and disease when Adam and Eve ate the forbidden fruit of knowledge. The picture of the world creating itself in response to God's call is more joyful, more miraculous—and much more accurate in describing what actually occurred.

Death is not the result of a curse, but an intrinsic part of the process of natural creation. Contrary to the Genesis account, the fossil record shows that organisms have died from the beginning of life's evolution, long before the first humans appeared. Death has allowed the continuous development of living things and their amazing variety.

Our next section explains how pain, suffering, and death have played a foundational role in the development of life, a process further discussed in Appendix A. Later, in Chapter 6, we'll examine at length one of the great problems in traditional belief: how a good and loving God, who is also omnipotent and omniscient, could create a world where that is so.

Emergence

There is one more significant concept related to evolution and the cosmos that we'd like to address: emergence, the process by which larger entities and patterns arise through interactions among smaller or less complicated entities that do not exhibit these characteristics on their own. Emergence describes how everything in the cosmos came to be and continues to become—from the initial Big Bang to the first interconnected atoms to the evolution of the first single-celled organism to whatever the future may hold. Emergence explains how the first *Homo* species came to have a brain complex enough to evolve a concept of the sacred. It explains why, at some point, some of these early ancestors of ours attributed sacredness to the rivers that brought them water, fish, and other beautiful, life-sustaining gifts, and how others first breathed "Tao" or "Om," or whispered "Yahweh" or "my God" to describe their experience of an unknowable otherness.

It also explains the negative aspects of the earliest religions. Our ancestors' deities were not only life-giving and awe-inspiring, but also arbitrary and severe—like unharnessed nature. When a flood or drought or other natural disaster occurred, these ancient believers assumed it was an "act of God" or the gods—punishment for a sin they had committed. And in their negative as well as their positive manifestations, these shared beliefs encouraged and reinforced group cooperation—an extremely successful evolutionary advantage.

Our Tribal Inheritance, for Better or Worse

The process by which group cooperation developed also explains why our species tends to cling so tenaciously to its ancient creation myths. As the first human tribes emerged, a new kind of evolution, cultural evolution, began to supplement genetic evolution as a factor in the success or failure of humans and other species among the "higher" animals. Cultural evolution played a larger and larger role in the development of these complex organisms, and in *Homo sapiens* it became the dominant influence.

For example, when early human cultures began engaging in the agriculture that gave them a more stable source of food, they began to pass on the emotional and intellectual traits that enabled them to work cooperatively together as a group. Concepts developed—loyalty, trust, self-sacrifice—that caused individuals to favor the needs of the group and in turn enabled the group to take better care of its individual members and thus to survive. More and more, survival came to depend on social learning, shared cultural assumptions, and beliefs and practices that were passed on from generation to generation.

This may well be the evolutionary reason that we tend to hold on so obstinately to literal belief in our ancient creation myths. The Harvard biologist Edward O. Wilson, for example, has written extensively on the evolutionary reasons that in-group loyalty, including loyalty to the religion of a culture, increases the likelihood of a group's survival.[8]

The same trait that prompted virtuous behavior within the tribe, however, also "justified" the extermination of rival tribes and food competitors, whom the tribe saw as "the other." In fact, hatred of "the other" was often encouraged to reinforce tribal cohesion. Out-group hostility, like in-group loyalty, is deeply imprinted in our genetic heritage.

Fortunately, humanity has made some progress in this area. As we continued to evolve, our ancestors entered into cooperative relationships with ever larger groups: first villages, then small kingdoms, then nations, and on to today's global markets, international governmental and nonprofit organizations, and the World Wide Web that connects us all. Unfortunately, our progress has not been all forward; we have stumbled and strayed backward more than once in our long history. We are in a retrograde period now, with racism and bigotry resurging in America, and civil wars and wars of unlawful conquest being fought around the globe. Further, powerful interests are resisting the measures needed to stave off climate disaster, famine, and the spread of disease.

But we can no longer afford to slide back so far. Our species has come to dominate the entire planet, and its quarreling tribes now have an arsenal of weapons of mass destruction at their disposal. It is obvious that the "in-group" mindset is much more dangerous today than it was when we fought with spears and clubs. And now that human economic activity has altered the global climate, our survival will depend on worldwide cooperation more than ever. Like it or not, we will have to become one tribe.

God: A Human-Constructed Emergence, or Something More?

There is one thing the theory of emergence doesn't tell us. Those experiences of the sacred, those gods that our ancestors described—are they strictly human-constructed, like our cultures and our systems of commerce? Are they fictions that were invented to explain things our ancestors didn't understand? Or do those words describing divinity that have come down to us over centuries and millennia point to an actual energy, spirit, or being that humans were able to experience and speak about after they became conscious—an ineffable something that is more than a human construction?

Scientists point out that from the Big Bang onward, complexity has always emerged from simpler states of being. The first energy, quarks, and electrons gave rise to the first atoms and elements, which led to the first gasses, stars, and planets, and eventually to Earth, where microorganisms gradually evolved into the first primitive plants and animals. Eventually, through billions of evolutionary twists and turns, those primitive precursors gave rise to today's incredible network of complex organisms, including our own species.

Thus, they argue, there couldn't have been a divinity with consciousness, intelligence, and love at the beginning of the universe; such complexity at the start of the cosmos would completely contradict all the evidence on how creation works. Furthermore, they insist, there's absolutely no evidence that some divine being intelligently designed the universe, including Earth's creatures. In addition, they say, religious historians have pointed out that the world's various deities conform amazingly well with the history and worldview of the cultures in which people first began to believe in them.

Therefore, say nontheists, God must be a human invention. It is not at all surprising that humans would invent God, based on the numerous evolutionary adaptations that have enabled humans to thrive. For example, the first members of the genus *Homo* who recognized that other creatures saw the world from a different point of view, and who could use their mental representations of that point of view in order to anticipate how those other creatures would behave, were better able to avoid predators and find prey. Those are the *Homo* species that survived and reproduced and evolved into *Homo sapiens*, "wise humans."

Our early ancestors recognized that other humans and animals had "agency," that they were capable of independent thought and action. From this observation, it isn't surprising that they would also attribute agency to the rivers and rain, and the sun, stars, and planets. After all, these entities seemed to be doing things that were sometimes beneficial for the tribe, and sometimes not, and they must have reasons for their actions. If they were indeed agents, then, presumably, they could be influenced to act in ways that the tribe desired. Perhaps they'd like a meal of freshly cooked meat, such as humans offered one another as a gesture of goodwill? Such "burnt offerings" were common in many early religious systems. A shared belief system based on the sacred also enhanced tribal cohesiveness and loyalty—another evolutionary advantage for survival.

Not Merely Superstition

But not all speculation about the nature of the divine is simply tribal superstition. For example, the atheists who argue that God is a human construction are invariably referring to a God who was complex from the beginning—a God who was fully formed, personal, and omnipotent, floating around in an eternity where there was nothing, and who suddenly created the world and the universe. A God, robed and white-bearded, whose mighty arm stretched out to bring Adam to life, exists only in the Sistine Chapel.

Yet although Michelangelo's Lord and all the many other Gods created in our image are human inventions, that does not mean there is not an actual Ground of All Being that all those anthropocentric concepts are attempting to describe. "Human invention" doesn't do justice to the deep mystical traditions shared by the world's largest religions—Christianity, Judaism, Hinduism, Islam, Buddhism, Taoism, and others. Nor do "primitive superstitions" exhaust the grandeur and immenseness of the beyond, the transcendent, the unknowable, that is the source of all that is. A universe with just us little humans as its pinnacle of consciousness, with no other God than the ones we invent, is, for many, far too small.

Again: Just because the superstitions of the ancients may no longer be credible, that doesn't mean there is no all-pervading mystery, no ultimate ground of being. It is one thing to say, "Here is the picture of God that my culture has taught me, and I'm going to live, speak, and think only inside this framework." It is very different to say, "I'm confronted with the possibility that the religious system I inherited from my parents and their parents is incomplete and parts of it are inadequate. Still, these beliefs may be pointing, however inadequately, toward some more ultimate reality. The words of the various traditions reach outward toward . . . not an Almighty Father figure with human attributes, but toward something that is so immense that I will never be able to entirely grasp it with my human mind."

If our ancient descriptions of God are actually naming something that is, but for which all names are inadequate, how do we find out more about that Something, or, for that matter, find the language to talk about it? How do we even begin to approach a conception of the sacred that is deep enough and comprehensive and subtle enough? These are the questions time and the progress of human knowledge have put before us, and they are not easy ones. Even today, many religious people resist exchanging Michelangelo's visualized, humanized, comprehensible God for that beyond-human Source, and either reject evolution altogether or seek a theory that softens and modifies it, such as Intelligent Design. And many atheists cling to the equally comforting idea that a purely material explanation for the final mysteries exists, and that we will find it someday. For readers especially interested in why many religious people still struggle with the science of evolution, we suggest a detour into Appendix A.

Biology and Evolution
An Existential Summary of Chapter 4

WE PAUSE HERE TO summarize what insight the above concepts of biology and evolution can give us into the questions of our existence:

- If you were to guess God's best-loved beings by their sheer quantity and staying power, you'd have to go with parasites. Parasites make up more than three-quarters of the world's species. They have been present since the early beginnings of life on Earth and they have also been among the major engines of evolution. After all, a species with a new mutation that enables it to survive an annoying or deadly pest is more likely to thrive, and new mutations often result in several unique new traits in addition to that pest resistance.

- Similarly, based on the evidence in nature, God really seems to like sex of all kinds—abusive, loving, creepy, intimate, grotesque, and even homicidal (think of the praying mantises that eat their "husbands" after mating with them)—as well as sexuality of all kinds: heterosexual, homosexual, transsexual, and transspecies. And asexuality: Think of the many kinds of self-reproducing bacteria, fungi, molds, hydras, and amoebae; the plants that clone themselves; the insects, crustaceans, and other creatures that are able to reproduce asexually as well as sexually, depending on the circumstances. Clearly, sexual reproduction—which produces descendants with the most variety—is the major motor of evolution. Still, you name it, and the plant and animal kingdoms have tried it. The methods of sex are staggeringly infinite, ranging from positively bizarre to truly tender. All of them together produce an infinite variety of offspring... most of which die before adulthood and never reproduce at all.

- Suffering is a major fact for all forms of life. As you read this sentence, countless animals are being eaten alive, dying from famine or parasites, or coming to other gruesome ends. Humans are not exempt. Whether we are good or evil makes no difference—it seems to be largely an accident of time, place, and the circumstances of our birth whether or not we are dealt a life of misery, good fortune, or something in between.

- Furthermore, our human species has created much of its own suffering throughout a history marred by war, genocide, rape, torture, slavery, inquisitions, and holocausts—all the violence we've used against individuals, tribes, and countries whom we defined as "the other."

- And in the past sixty years, with almost six thousand years of civilization under our belts, we have also caused the extinction of myriads of plant and animal species, and we are currently destroying many more, through the trash and pollution with which we fill our lands and oceans, and the climate change we cause with the carbon we spew into the air. Our nuclear weapons provide even more possibilities for destroying ourselves. If we continue at this pace, it is unlikely that humanity's reign will last anywhere nearly as long as the dinosaurs' 165 million years—we'll be lucky to make it to two hundred thousand.

* * *

On the other hand, our biological and evolutionary heritage have given us options that offer more promising outcomes:

- Our biology is not our sole destiny. Through religion, philosophy, law, convention, art, and literature, we have continually attempted to rise above the baser instincts and impulses, both individual and collective, which are also products of our evolutionary heritage.

- Thanks to civilization and technology, there is enough prosperity to support large numbers of seekers and idealists, who strive to orient us more toward the common good. The saints, religious and secular, the teachers and learners and discoverers, the altruists among us, in their words and actions, are working to make the world a place where the blind see, the lame walk, the prisoners go free, and the poor and oppressed have a shot at a better lot in life, so that we and the yet-unborn generations of Earth's species have a chance to thrive and grow in a sustainable future.

- We are all interrelated: The structure of our DNA and the fossil records show that all humans are kin to one another and to every other living thing—to the stars, the galaxies, to everything in the universe, whose elements we share.

- Cooperation is key for evolutionary success. Cooperation is one of the most common survival traits in nature across all species, and many of our core religious values—love one another, treat others as we'd like to be treated—make biological sense as well. We have always had profound emotions like romantic love, as well as feelings of charity and generosity toward those in need, that inspire altruistic and admirable behavior, and there are strong, positive evolutionary reasons for this.

- Life, as found in nature, seems to glory in variety, novelty, complexity, and intimacy. If humanity as we know it today came to an end, it is not unlikely that a new highly intelligent species would eventually emerge. We tend to believe that the world is better off with *H. sapiens* in charge instead of other earlier and even contemporary hominids, such as the Neanderthals. But we could be wrong. What if gentler primates, such as bonobos, had developed advanced intelligence instead of us? They could have, given different environmental conditions, and the world might have been a far more peaceful place.

- And if an intelligent species were to arise more violent and brutal than we are, the evolutionary record of other species suggests that to have long-term success, they would eventually have to evolve the ability, and thus the will, to cooperate. In other words, science has taught us that the evolution of intelligent life includes a certain tendency toward love and cooperation.

- The humans and other intelligent species that developed on our planet are, as far as we know, very rare in our universe. We are all the more precious because our existence is improbable.

- Evolution also gives us a fantastic origin story—not a metaphor, but a true history. Connie Barlow—science writer, evolutionary educator, and climate activist—puts it beautifully:

Part One: Creation: What We Now Know

Tell me a creation story more wondrous than that of a living cell forged from the residue of exploding stars. Tell me a story of transformation more magical than that of a fish hauling out onto land and becoming amphibian, or a reptile taking to the air and becoming bird, or a mammal slipping back into the sea and becoming a whale. Surely this science-based culture of all cultures can find meaning and cause for celebration in its very own cosmic creation story.[9]

- For humanity today, the story of evolution is about far more than just biological surviving, thriving, and reproducing. Because it helps us to understand where we have come from, it enables us to better address the issues that life on Earth is currently facing. Knowing the limitations that biology's trial-and-error progress has bequeathed to us allows us to work for a better future for all species, not just our own.

5

Our Big Brains & Why We Are the Way We Are

OUR LARGE, COMPLEX BRAINS are the most important evolutionary heritage that we enjoy as humans. They are the immediate source of our beliefs, our actions, our emotions, and our experience of the sacred. Understanding our brains' evolutionary past and their inner workings sheds tremendous light on issues relating to religion, responsibility, why we act the way we do, and what this might mean for our future.

As it turns out, this complicated and complex organ has an exceptionally convoluted and jury-rigged history. About 600 million years ago, our ancestors the first vertebrates emerged with three-part brains attached to their spinal cords. As primitive as these ur-brains were—and they were extremely primitive—they were a game-changer. The new species that had them were able to develop more successful ways of finding food and mates and avoiding predators, thanks to one specialized clump of neurons that handled unconscious functions like breathing and heartbeat, another clump that controlled posture and movement, and a third that directed sensory organs.

Over time, various mutations caused additional clumps of neurons to emerge that enabled more complex behaviors, each clump added onto the previously existing structures. Well before the evolution of mammals, brains developed a new outer layer, called the limbic system, that included sections to control emotions and drives, hormonal activity, hunger, sleep, attachment behaviors, memory, and more.

The Rise of the Mammals

After the dinosaurs died off, mammals began to increase in size, which vastly increased the incidence of further mutations, leading to a much larger and more complex variety of mammalian brains. Many of these mutations were not advantageous, and the mammals that had them did not thrive. But others gave their possessors a considerable edge in survival, bonding, and reproduction, and the new mammal species that resulted began spreading. Social instinct—the tendency to cooperate and form attachments in a group larger than a nuclear family—was one such evolved characteristic.

Primates—our precursors—and other social mammals developed another layer of neurons covering the limbic system, called the allocortex, and then eventually the neocortex. These even more complex brains allowed them to think and plan ahead instead of simply responding to immediate situations. They could now recognize that other animals had their own points of view, and they began to adapt their behavior to what they knew these other creatures could see and not see. Larger brains also allowed the mammals to try out scenarios in advance: if I do this, they'll probably do that. Of course, if you know that a particular action is likely to kill you, you're unlikely to take it. You live longer that way.

Our Contradictory Drives

The conflicting systems in our brains and nervous systems have each conferred evolutionary advantages, which helps explain the conflicting drives we have. Frequently our more primitive impulses urge us to do things that our reason tells us are flat-out stupid, and yet often enough, we do them anyway.

At the dawn of human civilization, this battle between reason and desire was a mystery. The ancients knew nothing of evolution or neuroscience. In order to explain their own complex and often contradictory behavior, they created stories and metaphors: angels and devils whispering in their ears; serpents tempting them to eat forbidden fruit; gods, spirits, demons, and demigods influencing them in various and often conflicting ways.

Early Humans Had Different Forms of Consciousness than We Do

In fact, when the creators of these stories claimed to hear the voices of gods, it is highly likely they believed they had. The late psychologist Julian Jaynes was one of the first to suggest that the ancients didn't yet have the perception to differentiate between the voices in their head—their thoughts—and outside voices.

He proposed that even though our brains are almost identical, our consciousness today is different from that of these distant ancestors, and possibly came into being only 2,500 to 3,000 years ago. That's an amazing hypothesis, if you think about it. One of the pieces of evidence he gave was that in *all* of the most ancient stories, including those in the *Odyssey* and the earliest books of the Bible, the gods set the stories in motion rather than the humans. For example, the Israelites, led by Joshua, believed God told them to slaughter every Canaanite man, woman, and child, so the Israelites could seize their land "flowing with milk and honey." And Paris, prince of Troy, believed the goddess Aphrodite told him to travel to Sparta to take Helen as his wife while Helen's husband was away in Crete.

The Dutch metaphysics and philosophy professor Jan Sleutels took Jaynes's idea a step further when he coined the term "Flintstones Fallacy." *The Flintstones* was a cartoon series from the 1960s that assumed its Stone Age characters, Fred and Wilma Flintstone and Barney and Betty Rubble, had the same ways of thinking and same consciousness that we do. That, Sleutels says, is a fallacy. Sleutels and other scientists and philosophers argue that ancient worldviews were radically different from ours, and that the human consciousness that produced them has likely changed significantly since then as well, even though their brain structure was not radically different from ours.[10]

And yet some of those ancient stories and viewpoints have had tremendous staying power. Not surprisingly, most of the stories that have stuck with us through the ages have echoes from our evolutionary history.

Echoes in Evolution

Take the tree of the knowledge of good and evil. According to Genesis, God told Adam and Eve not to eat its fruit, so they would not acquire its godlike knowledge. When a sneaky serpent sweet-talked the couple into trying the famous apple, the story says, the first two humans suddenly knew right from wrong.

Their innocence lost, they became aware that their nudity was something to be ashamed of, and covered themselves. They also understood that disobeying God's command concerning the tree was wrong, and hid from God. God, in turn, punished them by banning them from the Garden of Eden, where they had been living in ignorant, innocent bliss. No wonder this story has staying power—it is a metaphor for the evolutionary progress of our species.

All basic animal functions are driven by instinct: breathing, sleeping, fighting, fleeing, and reproducing. Animals with less-developed brains appear to be limited to those instinctive behaviors, doing what they must to survive without having any consciousness of moral choice, at least in any form we can recognize. Moral choice or reason as we know it only emerged in animals with more advanced prefrontal cortexes—including our species.

Humans eventually developed a very complex awareness of the different consequences of our actions, leading to the knowledge that some actions are better and some worse. As a result, we began ascribing values to our actions, calling them loving or selfish, heroic or base. From an evolutionary perspective, this is how we acquired the knowledge of good and evil. Before that, our ancestors were technically innocent, even when they engaged in behaviors that today we would consider evil.

Stories like Adam and Eve's fall, Cain and Abel, and Noah and the flood helped tribal members better understand human actions and interactions. Back then, however, the morality was usually black and white, often frightfully so: Israel's enemies = Evil; Israelites = Good. Therefore genocide of their enemies by Israelites in order to take their lands = Good.

Today, the knowledge of our evolutionary heritage and new breakthroughs in neuroscience enable us to explain why we are the way we are in a much deeper and richer way than was possible then. These discoveries also help us understand our own failings, so we can deal with them more effectively, and be more sympathetic toward the shortcomings of others as well.

Consider the seven deadly sins—lust, gluttony, avarice, sloth, wrath, envy, and pride. They are our primitive drives, the impulses from the limbic system that fight with our more rational neocortex. They are classic examples of Jesus's lament that "the spirit is willing, but the flesh is weak."[11] In his own way, Paul understood that there is something in basic human nature that makes it very hard to be a saint.

We struggle to stay with one partner at a time today because our ancestors who acted on their strong sex drives (Lust) were the ones who produced the most offspring, and thus came to dominate their species and later their society. Without this sexual drive, the human species wouldn't exist. And that's an important point to remember: Just because our limbic system is more primitive than our neocortex doesn't make it entirely bad. Along with our sex drive, the limbic system contributes to feelings of attachment, which play a crucial role in commitment. The hormones that produce attachment, combined with the voice of reason from our neocortex, help parents stay together for the good of their relationship and their children, in spite of occasional lustful feelings for others, or wrathful feelings toward each other.

Instincts versus Actions:
Readjusting the Definition of "Sin"

This is one case where current knowledge suggests it is time for some readjustments to the traditional religious classifications of sin. Having "lustful desires" is not a sin; it is instinct. Acting on those desires in harmful ways is wrong, a "sin," because we have not only instinct to drive us but also reason to restrain us. In fact, we even have a limbic drive on the side of good: attachment, the instinct to not harm those whom we care for and depend on, and who depend on us—our mate, our children, our community. But to define lust itself as a sin is misguided and produces unnecessary guilt. It represents a misunderstanding of how our brains and hormones work. Sexual thoughts and desires are just a normal part of being human. Focusing on lust and giving in to it in ways that hurt yourself or others is the sin.

Likewise, we all know we should avoid unhealthy food and overeating. Yet we tend to crave sugar, fat, and salt. It is not just because of a constant barrage of junk-food advertising. Gluttony, too, is a normal part of being human. Early humans whose drives caused them to gorge on food when it was plentiful were less likely to die of starvation when food was scarce, because they were the ones with more fat stored in their bodies. Sweets like honey from a wild hive or fat from a successful kill were especially good at providing extra calories, as well as minerals and proteins that early humans normally didn't get. Salt not only helped replenish electrolytes after exertion, but it also preserved food from rotting, and the humans who craved it were likely the first to discover its usefulness in preserving food.

So in ancient times, our ancestors who craved fat, salt, and sugar were more likely to survive. And yet, as we all know only too well, those who indulge these cravings today are likely to die sooner than those who do not. Interestingly, only after agriculture developed (giving humans a food source, grain, that could be stored against times of scarcity) was gluttony identified as a sin. In fact, according to Daniel 1 in the Old Testament, Daniel and his friends thrived by eating a vegetarian diet instead of the wine and rich food offered in the Babylonian court.

The "sinful" instincts of the body—gluttony and lust—are easy enough to ascribe to the limbic system. But there are also evolutionary causes for the more complicated "sins" of the mind, such as envy. (There are also evolutionary causes for cooperative behaviors; more on that shortly.)

In prehuman primate societies, such as monkey tribes, members already differed from one another in status. Those with higher status had greater power and access to interested mates. So the drive for high status—along with all the emotions, characteristics, and behaviors that serve that drive, including anxiety over the high status attained by others—appeared in primates early on as a survival trait.

Envy remains with us today, still serving its ancient purpose. Our desire to "keep up with the Joneses" spurs us to get good grades, work hard, plan our future, hit the gym, or finish our first novel. And sometimes, unfortunately, to tattle, backstab, or undermine a rival's success. So when envious feelings surface, we can acknowledge them and understand them for the primitive feelings they are, move on, and wish the person we envy well, instead of feeling guilty.

An Ethical Assist from Science

Imagine: Scientific understanding of ourselves, far from making us less moral, less reverent toward things of the spirit, can actually assist us in the ethical and spiritual quest. If we understand our impulses toward greed, sloth, wrath, and pride as entirely normal, we have more power to address them in constructive ways, rather than feeling guilty for having them or, even more harmfully, trying to ignore and suppress them.

Knowing the evolutionary nature of our brain and its conflicting desires also puts to rest the problematic assertion that it is God who tempts us. In other words, if you believe God created everything, you have to believe God tempts us. After all: Who made food that tempts us to be gluttons?

Who made pleasurable sex that tempts us to adultery? Who made alcohol intoxicating? Science offers understanding for the "sins" of temptation for which religion unfairly blames us, or for which we unfairly blame God.

Philo of Alexandria is said to have told his followers, "Be kind, for everyone you meet is fighting a great battle." When we realize there are strong evolutionary reasons for the conflicting pulls we so often experience, we can relax and begin to forgive both others and ourselves. When we accept ourselves for who we are, we can devise more realistic methods of addressing the problems we face, as individuals and as a species, in our homes, our communities, and our world.

Are We Just Biological Machines?

No debate in all of science more deeply affects our sense of who we are than the debate about consciousness and the brain. Many cognitive scientists and philosophers make the case that the perpetual battles going on in our minds—indeed, *all* of our thoughts and actions—are nothing more than nerve synapses, brain chemicals, and reactions. We are, they say, simply biological machines. Extremely sophisticated, of course, but still basically machines. As a (not-to-be-named) neurologist once told his audience at a conference, "Wires and chemicals, that's all we are—wires and chemicals."

Our brains have about 86 billion neurons, a significant proportion of the roughly 37 trillion cells in the human body. (These numbers are based on extrapolations and may not be very accurate. We won't even speculate about the numbers of synapses for each neuron.)

If we were shrunk to microscopic size and could travel among our own cells and observe all the activity, it would appear to be complete pandemonium. Yet it is actually highly organized communication. These countless interactions are what cause us to think, act, react, plan, and make sense of each other and our world. They also make us the kind of people we are.

Of course, most of us think we are more than machines. We believe we have some essence—call it consciousness, call it soul, call it the self—that makes us more than the sum of our parts and processes. We experience what it is to be a self, and the most sophisticated computer does not. All these instincts and unconscious brain processes somehow produce people who love and dream and create and reflect—when all is going well, of course. Out of the whole process emerges the richness of the human spirit.

PART ONE: CREATION: WHAT WE NOW KNOW

What, Then, Is the Human Spirit?

It is only recently that fMRI and PET scans from neuroimaging have allowed an explosion of knowledge about the correlations between mental states and specific brain processes. Before that, most people believed that there was some kind of "ghost in the machine." Whether they called it spirit or soul, it seemed to presuppose some little guy inside the head, conscious of everything occurring within us and making free decisions about what the body should do. As hard as it may be to give it up, that picture just doesn't make sense anymore, given what we now know about the brain.

And yet . . . you don't have to leap from the latest issue of the *Annals of Neurology* to the conclusion that we are "nothing but" our brain processes. Perhaps a God didn't physically insert a soul into the proto-you the moment that your parents' sperm and egg formed a fertilized ovum. But why should not harboring such an entity mean that we are "nothing but" our brain processes? The wonder of human existence is that out of the complex body-and-brain that we are, amazing qualities of goodness and nobility and compassion can emerge. To be a person is to be much, much more than "wires and chemicals."

However, a tremendous amount of current neuroscience and cognitive science appears to validate the claims of those who view us as biological machines. If they are right, for example, you would expect that the state of our neurons would directly affect our thoughts and emotions. It certainly does.

Changing our Brain Chemistry Changes Us

When we subject our brains to various drugs, drinks, and vapors, we can feel high, sleepy, alert, inhibition-free, trippy, hyper, irritable, sluggish, and so on. Certain hallucinogens can make us feel that we are transcending our self and becoming at one with the world; others may give us terrifying nightmares. Incredibly, thanks to modern brain imaging, we can now get pictures of what exactly is happening in a person's brain as various parts of it are "lit up" by the firing of neurons. We can't see *what* that person is thinking or feeling, but we can see the brain processes, impaired or enhanced, that are occurring *while* they are thinking or feeling it.

Meditation can also influence the actions of our neurons. Neuroimaging shows differences in neurological patterns between experienced meditation practitioners and control groups consisting of nonmeditators.

Brain changes have been measured across a wide variety of traditions, including Tibetan Buddhist monks, Franciscan sisters, and experienced nonreligious meditators.[12] Although neuroscientists find significant differences in brain activation between practitioners in different traditions, they also consistently discover sharp contrasts between those with a serious practice of meditation or prayer and those without such a practice. The feelings of centeredness, peace, and reduced stress experienced by seasoned meditators have inspired the current Western trend of "mindfulness training" that is now a common practice.

The brain chemistry we were born with and brain changes that may occur during our life also influence our thoughts and emotions. For example, lesions in the lower temporal lobe can cause a marked increase in religious experiences, and certain synthetic chemicals can cause ecstatic visions and hallucinations. Some of these experiences produce an increased sense of awe, beauty, and reverence that may last for years. Such unusual brains may have produced many of the religious visions and epiphanies experienced by saints and mystics of old, some of whom became the founders of our major religions.

There are a multitude of other chemical changes that produce less positive states of mind, such as autism, depression, psychosis, and more. Brain imaging illuminates these impaired states as well. You can understand why Alzheimer's patients have trouble processing information and accessing memories, for example, when you see the plaques that disrupt the neurons in their brains.

In extreme cases, brain disruptions can transform a person's character. In *The Happiness Hypothesis*, psychologist Jonathan Haidt writes of a schoolteacher suddenly becoming a remorseless rapist and child molester. When the man went to the emergency room because of a pounding headache just before he was to be tried for his crimes, doctors discovered a huge tumor on his frontal cortex and removed it. Immediately, the teacher was restored to his normal, good, responsible self. When the tumor grew back, so did his criminal sexual mania, until it was removed a second time, and his terrible symptoms disappeared for good.[13]

Should the teacher be held accountable for the actions that he committed under the influence of the tumor? Many people would say that in spite of the terrible consequences suffered by his victims, he should not be locked up for the rest of his life. After all, without a functioning frontal cortex, he had no way of differentiating between good and evil. The tumor had caused him to revert to the state of most of the rest of animal creation, which operates on instinct without a consciousness of right and wrong. That consciousness, it turns out, depends on the brain functioning in a particular way.

This brings up a major question: Are any of us completely responsible for our actions?

Do We Even Have Free Will?

Many cognitive scientists and philosophers who study the mind make the case that free will is an illusion. Even though we may seem to ourselves to have free will, they say, everything we do is actually determined—by our DNA, brain chemistry, environment, and other factors.[14]

By using this information neuroscientists can make particular and localized predictions about a subject's behavior, and even an ordinary person who knows another person well can often predict what that other person would likely do in many typical situations. Only an omniscient being could predict what a given person would do in every situation. Therefore, the prospect of disproving free will by predicting all of a person's actions doesn't look too promising.

Whether or not humans have some degree of genuinely free will appears to be one of those "metaphysical" questions—one just as difficult to prove or disprove as whether or not God exists. So far, we are unable to resolve such questions empirically. Since the data are currently inconclusive, that leaves it up to you to decide whether you prefer to think of yourself as free or not—which, we admit, sure *sounds like* a free decision . . .

Faith in Free Will

So, viva free will! Unless you have a tumor growing on your frontal cortex, like the unfortunate teacher turned rapist, or some other brain impairment that prevents you from being responsible for your actions, you are free to view yourself, and the vast number of people around you, as having moral agency. In fact, such agency may well be the most important kind of freedom of all.

We can't demonstrate that we enjoy unconstrained freedom from all determining factors. Nor can we show that we are free in a metaphysical sense by proving that we have some unique soul or energy or essence that makes us "really" free. It *could* be that we are just machines, that freedom is an illusion, and that consciousness is just a predictable byproduct of our neural machinery, like the heat your car engine generates when you run it.

But . . . our sophisticated brains have produced some amazing emergent properties, like Hogwarts and *Hamlet* and Beethoven's Ninth Symphony. So it is just as likely—and actually, we think, *more* likely—that our complex brains have helped us to become persons: morally responsible agents who are able to consider the wishes and needs of others instead of just attending to our own. People who can do this are able to act for the benefit of the broader community.

So, it looks like a good bet to conclude that we are free, at least in the sense of possessing the personal and moral agency that we have defended here. Equally important, having this degree of freedom means we are capable of transcending some of the negative aspects of our evolutionary heritage.

Our Biology Is Not Our Destiny

Evolutionary history is neither moral nor immoral. It is simply the process through which certain species survive and others die out. It favors fecundity, no matter what. In some species, reproductive methods have evolved that would seem horrifying if they were ours. Female praying mantises sometimes eat their mates, even biting off their heads while they copulate, and the mantis is an evolutionary success. But that doesn't mean spouse killing (let alone spouse cannibalism) would be a good survival strategy for humans.

Mantises are amoral. By and large, humans are moral. We have evolved to the point where (at least sometimes) we freely and consciously choose our actions. We are also social animals, since cooperative relations with others are central to our lives and survival. That's why ethics and morality lie at the very core of our existence and our sense of ourselves.[15]

We can encourage traits, such as empathy and cooperation, that will take our species in the direction that will best help it to thrive in the future. We can also reject or discourage other traits, such as aggression, that once aided our survival but now threaten it. There are evolutionary reasons why humans are capable of great brutality, but we are not forced to behave brutally.

Understanding that evolution values fertility and survival above all else helps us to confront instincts and behaviors that have evolved within us. One thinks immediately of sexual and aggressive urges. But many other urges fall under this heading as well: the urge to lie, to overeat fat and sugar, to feel jealous, and to mistrust people with a different skin color from our own.

Acting on these biological instincts may have contributed to our original success as a species, but doing so now is harmful for our interactions with each other and the world. Knowing where these urges came from can help us be more conscious of our feelings, to analyze them before we act on them. Truly, nobody is perfect, and knowing why that is so can free us from guilt and shame. It can also help us address our evolutionary strengths and weaknesses more thoughtfully and productively. This knowledge even provides clues about how we can harness the power of our primitive drives for more constructive purposes, and gives us insight for leading more accepting and fulfilled lives.

Evolutionary biologist David Sloan Wilson pointed this out:

> Our unique attributes evolved over a period of roughly 6 million years. They represent modifications of great ape attributes that are roughly 10 million years old, primate attributes that are roughly 55 million years old, mammalian attributes that are roughly 245 million years old, vertebrate attributes that are roughly 600 million years old, and attributes of nucleated cells that are perhaps 1,500 million years old. If you think it is unnecessary to go that far back in the tree of life to understand our own attributes, consider the humbling fact that we share with nematodes (tiny wormlike creatures) the same gene that controls appetite. At most, our unique attributes are like an addition onto a vast multiroom mansion. It is sheer hubris to think that we can ignore all but the newest room.[16]

Good Public Policy Takes Evolution into Account

In fact, we ourselves and society as a whole are much better served when we consciously take into account our evolutionary weaknesses as we design public policy.

As an example, consider the all-too-common problem of abuse of power. Baron John Dalberg-Acton clearly understood human nature when he wrote, in 1887, "Absolute power corrupts absolutely."[17] There are strong evolutionary reasons for the human tendency to desire more and more power. An increase in status and power raises testosterone levels in male primates (including male humans), which in turn inclines these successful males to more risk-taking, infidelity, and aggression, and more power grabbing.

It is important to acknowledge this fact, and then to make sure that systems are in place to deal with it. A perfect example of an institution that disregards our evolutionary heritage is the United States Congress. Predominantly male and possessing exceptional power and amazing levels of entitlement, lawmakers are encouraged to take optional anti-sexual harassment training (mandatory training was voted down). In spite of that option, every year legislators from both parties get caught in harassment and other sexual scandals. Active nonviolence training, in order to channel aggressive instincts into diplomatic techniques, would also be helpful.

This tendency is not limited to politicians. For example, the power-stimulated increase in testosterone levels is seen in religious as well as secular leaders. Prominent pastors and televangelists have been disgraced by sexual affairs after spending years publicly proclaiming their morality. Our legislators—even those who write anti-sexual harassment laws—are not immune to the effects of their own power and, like those famous preachers, have had scandals of their own come to light. In general, our Congress—which, among other things, is empowered to declare war—could benefit hugely from training in self-awareness and self-restraint, to counter the increased aggression that is a natural byproduct of their position.

Next Step: Playing God

There is another evolutionary reason that our biology is not our destiny. We not only have the ability to make moral choices; we also have the ability to make intellectual discoveries and to invent. Our earliest discoveries—agriculture, fire-making, the wheel—began the process of channeling our development and shaping our species, both biologically and socially. In modern times, that process has accelerated dramatically with our rapidly expanding knowledge on every subject and our amazing advances in technology. It is channeling our evolution in new and more radical directions.

In the past century, medicine has almost brought one form of human natural selection to a screeching halt, at least in developed nations. Thanks to the identification of germs and parasites with the diseases they cause, and the discovery of vaccines to prevent and drugs to treat them, we no longer have to die of those diseases that killed our ancestors. Naturally occurring mutations that might otherwise have conferred immunity or resistance to those diseases gradually lost their special importance to survival.

As a result, cultural evolution and technological progress have outpaced biological selection as the dominant forces determining the future of our species. Those of us who lose our sight, limbs, hearing, or various vital functions can become bionic humans of sorts with new limbs, new eyes, new ears, or new organs. Brain enhancement research has begun, and artificial intelligence (AI) expertise is growing rapidly. Brain sensors and electrodes now allow quadriplegic persons to control computer screens and artificial limbs by thought alone. The first stages of transhumanity—"trans" in the sense of transcending, as we rise above or overcome at least some of the strongest forces that controlled us in the past—are already upon us.

Beyond Biological Selection

While AI and robotics haven't proceeded as rapidly as we originally expected they might, both are steadily progressing, as are other new technologies.

Eventually the doctors and computer scientists will be creating more and better enhancements for our bodies and minds, governments will subsidize and control their inventions, cybercriminals and rebels will arise to thwart that work or use it for their own ends, and so on. Each of these groups will eventually enjoy powers once thought to be the exclusive province of gods.

Scientists are also rapidly developing more sophisticated techniques with CRISPR, a molecular gene editor developed in 2012 that is currently being used by researchers at all levels, including in undergraduate research laboratories. Our neighbor, Elizabeth Glater, a professor at Pomona College, has been working on *C. elegans*, which has genes similar to those of humans, even though it possesses an extremely simple nervous system of only 302 neurons. She and her team of undergraduate researchers are seeking to understand how genes and environment modify the nervous system to produce different food preferences.

Professor Glater cites promising early studies that use CRISPR to edit the human genome in an effort to study and, perhaps eventually, to treat sickle cell disease, which causes severe pain and premature death in millions of people worldwide. Scientists have already used CRISPR to remove the mutation that causes sickle cell disease in a mouse model, and are working toward clinical trials in humans. When the clinical trials are approved, scientists will remove blood stem cells from a patient with sickle cell disease, edit the genome of those cells to remove the sickle cell mutation, and then reinsert the modified cells into the person's bone marrow. Since there are still no cures for sickle cell disease, such a genome-editing approach could be a major advance. However, it is currently illegal to alter human embryos with CRISPR (although it was done illegally by one scientist in China, He Jiankui).[18]

Are We Evolved Enough to Meet These Challenges?

"We have created a *Star Wars* civilization, with Stone Age emotions, medieval institutions, and godlike technology," warns biologist Edward O. Wilson. "We thrash about. We are terribly confused by the mere fact of our existence, and a danger to ourselves and to the rest of life."[19] Is that where it will end—with a mammal whose brain was not quite big enough to keep it from destroying itself? Or will we evolve the moral and spiritual capacities, and the character, to make wise choices and to create a sustainable future for ourselves and our planet?

In many ways, the perilous era in which we now live represents a coming of age for our species. It is both exhilarating and frightening. This new era requires a level of ethical responsibility we've never had before. It has spiritual implications as well. Like it or not, we now have the ability to play god—over each other, over creation, and over the future of our planet. And we are woefully unprepared for our new quasi-divine status. Science isn't enough.

What we desperately need are helpful and centering spiritual practices, inspirational myths and rituals, and evolving religious traditions that are adequate to the twenty-first century . . . and beyond. We'll have to rely on more sophisticated ethical systems and ways of thinking, to make sure the transhuman phase that lies ahead of us proceeds in beneficial directions. We also need supportive communities that will help us use our new powers wisely and come to grips with the constantly evolving sense of who we are.

Neuroscience
An Existential Summary of Chapter 5

WE PAUSE HERE TO summarize what insight the above concepts of neuroscience can give us into the questions of our existence:

- Scientific understanding of ourselves, far from making us less moral, can actually assist us in our own ethical and spiritual quest. If we understand our impulses toward greed, sloth, wrath, and pride as entirely normal evolutionary instincts, we have more power to address them in constructive ways, rather than feeling guilty for having them or, even more harmfully, trying to ignore or deny them. We can accept ourselves for who we are, and devise more realistic methods of addressing the problems we face, as individuals and as a species.
- Today there are two possible futures for humanity. We disappear, destroyed by some combination of human-induced catastrophes such as a nuclear holocaust, mass sterility from the increasing number of chemicals we're putting into our environment, or the extreme effects of global warming and pollution, which have already begun causing mass extinctions of other species. Or . . . we survive into the distant future, because we rise to the challenges that face us. We accept the fact that we hold the key to the future survival of our species and the continuance of Earth's evolutionary processes. And we take collective responsibility for that future and stop elevating humans at the expense of our planet's millions of other species. Eventually, our technology may enable us to colonize other parts of space in preparation for the

time, approximately 7 billion years from now, when our Sun has become a red giant and begun consuming its closest planets. This optimistic scenario may eventually be possible, because, however slowly and irregularly, humanity has made crucial moral progress in the past.

- Our past shows a general trend toward the common good. As history has advanced, human circles of care and concern have expanded. At first, anyone outside your tribe was "the other." It was perfectly justifiable to slaughter, plunder, even devour outsiders who got in your tribe's way. But as our ancestors and their technologies evolved, they entered into cooperative relationships with ever larger groups—from villages to small kingdoms and finally to today's nations, which are connected by global markets, international governmental and private organizations, and the World Wide Web. Our survival no longer demands that we consider foreigners, nonbelievers, and outsiders as dangerous "others" to be disparaged, ostracized, or violently defeated.

- There will still be exceptions, of course: At the time this book is going to press, Russia is in the third year of a pointless and devastating war it launched unprovoked against its neighbor Ukraine; racism and white supremacy are openly espoused by more than a third of Americans; and wealthy and powerful individuals and corporations fight climate legislation as droughts, tornadoes, fires, melting glaciers, and other weather disasters wreak havoc on Earth and its species, including ourselves.

- At the same time, a global understanding is developing that we are all interrelated and interdependent. Nations and communities and groups are banding together to try to minimize the damage caused by counterproductive groups. We are slowly getting closer to embracing a worldwide solidarity, a solidarity that, as long as it is worldwide, cannot be based on the hatred of outsiders—because it leaves no one outside to hate. We are growing up and growing into the awareness that, as inhabitants of this "pale blue dot" in the heavens, we are and must be a global community.

- And that growth must accelerate if we are to use our powers to survive and save creation rather than devastate it. Whether our motive is religious or secular in origin, the necessity for sustaining our relations with each other and with all of life grows all the more urgent as humanity acquires more godlike powers in the world. We will soon be directly influencing our own development, transcending the biological limits of our bodies and minds and evolving at a much faster pace. This could produce a nightmare scenario, a blissful utopia, or, most likely, something in between. Much depends on the values that we as a species choose to guide our choices. The stakes are enormous.

So, where does all of this leave us? Some of our ancient foundational religious myths are not only prescientific but also antiscientific. And many of those who still believe them also still use them to support exclusivist, even violent tribal thinking. But isn't it also simplistic to therefore dismiss all religions as worthless? We will still need the resources of multiple religious traditions: inspirational narratives, rituals, moral teaching, ethical guidelines, and spiritual connections across human (and nonhuman) communities if we are going to establish a more sustainable civilization on this planet. Constructive reinterpretations of old stories and customs, inspiring new stories and traditions, and more adequate ways of speaking about God will all play an indispensable role in helping us cope with the constantly evolving world and the new versions of ourselves that we are co-creating.

- Many different future realities are possible, and our choices have a major role to play in the outcome. We have been gifted with the capacity to be co-actors and co-creators, with an amazing potential for affecting what comes next—to be partners with nature as we move forward with the opportunities that life gives us. Our sometimes brilliant, sometimes desperate and clumsy actions will launch this planet's evolutionary epic across yet another threshold, with major future consequences. It is a responsibility that is both scary and exhilarating.

Part Two

Religion Comes of Age

"We need myths that help us to venerate the earth as sacred once again, instead of merely using it as a 'resource.' This is crucial, because unless there is some kind of spiritual revolution that is able to keep abreast of our technological genius, we will not save our planet."

—Author Karen Armstrong

6

An Omnipresent God

MANY BELIEVERS STILL HOLD to a faith in a supernatural father figure—one who looks down from heaven to punish or bless us, depending on how we respond to his revelation and commandments. Centering on the transcendent, miracle-working God, however, can mean missing out on the more universal and deeper truths that our holy books reveal, as well as the realities uncovered by the groundbreaking discoveries of our era, truths that give greater insight into the fundamental questions of life.

The previous chapters, which examined current science for insight into these questions, have now set the stage. In this chapter we combine those insights with religion, philosophy, and reason to raise concerns about some of the older definitions of God.

The three great monotheistic religions, Judaism, Christianity, and Islam, have at various times all described God as present everywhere (omnipresent), all-powerful (omnipotent), all-knowing (omniscient), and entirely good (omnibenevolent).

Omnipresence easily fits with what we see in science and nature. At the most foundational quantum levels, matter, light, and energy are interrelated and interconnected, and all other relationships radiate outward from them. All of reality, then, is relational. These interwoven relationships co-create and influence all aspects of being—from quantum particles, through the ever-emerging variety of Earth's interdependent species, and out to the giant supernovas and stars at the farthest reaches of the universe that originally produced the elements of which we are made. It is not a big leap to conclude that if there is some kind of a divine essence, what many call God, it would be present in the relational forces, energies, and creativity that surge everywhere throughout the cosmos.

Aside from omnipresence, however, what we now know about science and the nature of things calls into question some of the other traditional assumptions about God's nature, especially the belief in God's unlimited omnipotence and all-controlling influence.

If God exists and is infinite, it does not follow that God must be understood as all-powerful as well. In fact, belief in an omnipotent God faces bigger challenges than not fitting with scientific knowledge. It does not fit with morality or good theology, either, especially since it conflicts with the even more foundational affirmation of God's goodness.

A Good God and an All-Powerful God Are Mutually Exclusive

Simply based on the evidence of the world we see around us, it seems highly unlikely that an all-good, all-powerful God supernaturally intervenes in the world on a regular basis. Too many innocent people suffer. Too many worthwhile prayers go unanswered.

Some believers reply that God *does* answer; God just often answers with a *no*. But this response is rather hard to swallow. Are we to say that God chose the Holocaust over other responses to prayer? Or that God has the power to prevent the abuse or torture of children but decides it is more redemptive to let them suffer? Or that "God's ways are not our ways," and therefore we should ignore our moral intuitions and trust that whatever terrible things occur, as awful as they may seem, are actually good? The cost of these responses to reason and morality is just too great.

The world contains countless examples of senseless suffering. When we think about some of the atrocious things that are done to innocent children, we rightly use the word "evil." If God is controlling a world filled with such abuse, that seems to make God responsible for the abuse.

Believers sometimes argue that what seems wrong to us might actually be right in the eyes of God. But that seems like a pretty high price to pay. If we are mistaken about our most fundamental moral beliefs—say, the belief that an innocent infant should not be made to suffer—then at least some of our deepest moral intuitions are wrong. It is hard to imagine how we could reliably navigate our way through the world as adult human beings if our moral compass is fundamentally inaccurate in this way.

Others respond that God has reasons for allowing the innocent to suffer; it is just that those reasons remain a mystery to us. Unfortunately, the appeal to mystery leaves us in the same place. It suggests that at least some of our core intuitions about right and wrong are mere illusions. God knows what's really right or wrong, but either keeps it a secret or knows that we couldn't understand the divine morality anyway. The result is the same in both cases: we now have reason to mistrust the moral and ethical intuitions that guide our actions, no matter how deep-rooted they may seem.

Faced with these difficulties, many believers take a different response. God is still all-powerful, able to cause anything to happen at any time, but God chooses not to be all-controlling. Sometimes God intervenes to work miracles in the world, directly bringing about the results that he wants. But at other times God refrains from intervening. In these cases, God is not responsible for the evil that then occurs; either natural laws are responsible, or the human being who does the evil action is responsible.

This belief in intermittent miracles, it turns out, brings problems of its own. The more you affirm these special interventions by God, these occasional miracles, the more God's noninterventions cry out for an answer. God has absolutely unlimited power and could effortlessly step in at any time to prevent horrendous evils that produce massive sufferings, but in fact God only intervenes from time to time. If that's true, then isn't God responsible for what happens when God does *not* intervene? Certainly we hold human parents to this standard; they are guilty of neglect when they ignore the needs of their children. Why would the same principle not apply to the heavenly Father as well?

Believers in an omnipotent God may reply that it is God's decision when to intervene and when not to, and it is not our place to question God's higher purposes. But this takes us right back to the problems with responses like "God's ways are not our ways," and "we just can't understand God's reasons." Both responses imply that our mature moral intuitions don't capture what really makes actions good or bad; only God knows those things.

To believe in an all-good God whose nature and actions are models for our ethical decision-making would be inspiring. But to be confronted by a God whose decisions go against our deepest moral intuitions, a God whose moral reasoning is completely opaque to us, undercuts any claim that we can reason reliably about right and wrong or act morally in the world around us.

Free Will Doesn't Solve the Problem

Let's consider one final argument that believers in omnipotence often make. Although God is all-powerful, they say, God is not all-controlling, for God doesn't always exercise his power. Sometimes God does not intervene in the natural order, because God wants to leave space for people to make their own choices. God refrains from acting just enough for humans (at least sometimes) to be free.

That still doesn't solve the problem, however. Imagine an all-powerful and all-good God, a God with infinite knowledge, who has absolutely unlimited ability to intervene in the world at any time to work miracles big and small. There are so many subtle ways that this God could decrease the suffering of the innocent, while still allowing humans to make free decisions. The world we see around us, with its atrocious unmitigated suffering, is not the kind of world one would expect to see if God is preventing evil as often as possible consistent with preserving human freedom.

The other problem that we encountered earlier raises its ugly head here as well, unfortunately. Imagine that God sometimes intervenes in the world out of compassion, and sometimes doesn't intervene in order to preserve human freedom. Yet, being all-powerful and all-knowing, God is actually able to do *something* in every case to decrease or eliminate suffering. Given this ability, any time that God doesn't do as much as possible to reduce innocent suffering, God has acted in a way that's inconsistent with being an omnipotent and all-good being.

A few examples will help to illustrate this point:

9/11

About a month after the 9/11 tragedy, many of us received an email that was circulating the Internet detailing the numerous ways God had saved various people from being in the Twin Towers that day: A baby had fallen ill, so the father or mother stayed home instead of going into work; a fender-bender delayed someone just the right amount of time; a late flight made someone miss a meeting; and on it went. The email thankfully praised God for saving all these people. Clearly, the people who forwarded it were inspired and thrilled by the idea of these divine "interventions."

However, what if you had lost a loved one in the 9/11 attacks and received this email? It would have been a slap in the face.

"What about my wife/husband/friend?" you would ask. Wasn't she or he worthy of being saved? If God is truly omnipotent, why didn't God save everyone? Why did God allow so many good, innocent people to die so young, and make so many children fatherless or motherless?

Two days after 9/11, on *The 700 Club* program, televangelists Jerry Falwell and Pat Robertson gave their answer. They informed us that God was intentionally allowing America's enemies to give us what we "likely deserved." If we didn't repent, they warned, God might even do worse to us. Falwell said he blamed the ACLU, the federal court system, abortionists, feminists, gays and lesbians, and all others who had angered God by trying to secularize America. Robertson emphatically agreed. They were right in one respect: *If* an all-powerful God would allow something so horrendous to happen, he must have had his reasons. Falwell and Robertson were just helping us all by pointing them out.

The Holocaust

Take it to another level of human-willed depravity: the Holocaust. Many who witnessed the atrocities of that era, especially those who managed to survive the concentration camps—where they had seen loved ones die of starvation, disease, beatings, and overwork, or rounded up to be murdered in the gas chambers—stopped believing in God altogether. They could not possibly fathom how an all-powerful, all-benevolent God could have allowed such extreme evil to triumph for so long. Compounding this evil, some people actually believe that the Jews must have deserved the punishment, or God wouldn't have let it happen. And it is not just anti-Semites who believe this.

In November 2013, Harvard's *Ichthus*, a student-run journal of Christian thought, published an online essay by an anonymous Jewish student who had become a Christian. In his article, this blogger said, "We, the Jews, rejected God and hung him up on a cross to die, and thus we richly deserved all of the punishments that were heaped on our heads over the last 2,000 years," and ended by urging all Jews to become Christians. When an uproar followed the publication of his blog, the *Ichthus* staff withdrew it and issued an apology.[20]

The unfortunate student, however, was simply following the logical conclusions of his beliefs: If God is indeed omnipotent, the terrible irony is that God really is responsible for your suffering . . . as well as for your victories, of course. If God is all-powerful and allows a horrible tragedy to befall you, then either you must have done something to deserve it (so you should feel guilty), or else God is capricious and neglectful, possibly even vindictive (so you may very well feel helpless).

Poverty

Poor and oppressed people, especially, often cling to a belief that God is all-powerful and entirely benevolent—hence, if they pray hard enough and follow God's directives, God will reward them by delivering them from their unhappy circumstances. Unfortunately, things usually don't work out that way. Then they wonder, if God is all-powerful and nonetheless leaves me in such dire straits, what went wrong? If God is all-powerful, why did he allow my beloved, innocent son or daughter with so much promise to be killed by a random bullet in a drive-by shooting? Was it my lack of faith? Was it my child's? Does God not care about us, but only about those who can afford to live in safe neighborhoods?

As long as one believes in a good God, capable of supernaturally intervening and choosing not to, there is no satisfactory theological answer to such questions. There are, however, logical explanations. For the poor especially: Many of the negative events in their lives are caused by their poverty. In fact, researchers have discovered that people who worry about where their next meal will come from make significantly worse decisions than they do when they, the same people, are in a more secure situation. When we are living in poverty, our cognitive load is increased by distracting tasks, stress, lack of sleep, and so on, impairing our capacity for decision-making, emotional regulation, and long-term planning. It is widely known that deprivation, chronic stress, and lack of reliable income can change the brain and the body in ways that reduce our ability to focus, learn, and succeed.

Believers in an omnipotent God may argue that a religion with a strong, black-and-white moral code and an all-powerful God motivates people in dire straits to make better decisions. If you fear a God of judgment or believe that God only helps those who are obedient, they argue, you'll be more likely to spend meager paychecks on family necessities instead of drink, drugs, affairs, gambling, and other harmful ways of escaping reality. Then you'll begin to acquire the tools and habits you need to enter the middle class.

In many places, however, that is not enough. When you live in an area with poor schools, a lack of jobs, gang-infested neighborhoods, corrupt officials, and so on, upward mobility will be difficult—even if you're a practicing believer. So, if you believe that there is a God who controls outcomes, who causes people to be in the place where he wants them to be, then you may think that he has arranged your life circumstances the way he wants them.

If you live in poverty and need, and if bad things happen to you and those you love, then God must want it that way. God is in complete control. "All things work together for good," but only "for those who love God" and "are called according to his purpose."[21] So if all things aren't working out in a good way for you, then presumably you don't love God enough, or perhaps you're not one of the ones who is called according to his purpose. Even if your omnipotent God, for the sake of preserving freedom or for some other reason, doesn't micro-manage the outcomes, this doesn't resolve the issue. You still face the difficult question of how an all-powerful, loving God can stomach such systemic poverty on such a vast scale, if he's really able to intervene at any time.

Lisa: A Case Study

In her book *Making a Way Out of No Way*, theology professor Monica A. Coleman tells of leading a weekly support group to help women victims of domestic violence muster the courage and get the support they needed to leave the abusive relationship. She tells of Lisa (not her real name), the mother of three young children, who arrived one night covered with bruises and with bald patches on her scalp, where her boyfriend had yanked out hunks of her hair while he was beating her. As they gathered around to comfort her, Coleman and another woman in the group began braiding her hair, to help her get fitted for a wig.

"Lisa," writes Coleman, "lived in a category lower than 'working class.' She was working a 39-hour-a-week job that left her tired enough to call it work but was one hour shy of health coverage; living in a housing project so unpredictable that taxi cabs refused to pick up or drop off after dark; and feeling emotionally dependent on a man who took her hair out by the fistful."[22]

Coleman writes that she wanted Lisa to understand "that her current reality was not her long-term fate; with support from my organization, the other women, our partners throughout the city and government, and a good dose of prayer, things could be different. I wanted to affirm that braiding patchwork hair was more than an act of compassion, that it might indeed be an act of salvation. I wanted to connect the specificity of her story with a worldview that acknowledges the reality of evil and loss and finds opportunities for life in each new moment without either waiting for God to make it happen or making Lisa do it all herself."

No omnipotent God had stepped in to save Lisa. It took women who were open to what they experienced as God's call to love, practiced caregivers who were also knowledgeable about social service agencies that could help Lisa address the severe problems she faced. It also took Lisa making herself open to these women to receive the help she needed.

We cannot affirm that an omnipotent God—one who regularly intervenes in the world to relieve unnecessary suffering—chose for Lisa to be born in the projects and grow up with the terrible level of abuse that she experienced. People in such situations are not responsible for the dismal circumstances into which they were born any more than those born with all the advantages in the world are responsible for their fortunate beginnings. An omnipotent God is not working behind the scenes to place each baby into exactly the situation they deserve, some into horrific, soul-shattering circumstances, and others into lives of leisure and unimaginable wealth.

But What About Miracles?

"But wait," some of you, the readers, are saying, "What about miracles and other things that seem impossible to explain by natural causes?"

We will address biblical miracles in Chapter 9, so that we can focus in this chapter on the contrasting images of God. For the moment, we simply note the observation by James F. McGrath of Butler University:

> To say that God once parted seas and flooded worlds and now helps Americans find parking spaces is, in my opinion, a move backwards and not forwards in our theological thinking. Indeed, that there are religious believers who will deal with the problem of evil by saying that God does not intervene to prevent genocides

and rapes and starvation on a grand scale in order to allow room for free will, but who will then thank God for intervening to get them a job or help them find a bargain at the mall, is not merely disturbing but truly sickening.[23]

If God Is Not All-Powerful, What Is the Point of God?

About now, many readers will certainly be asking: *If God is not omnipotent, then God's ability to influence the world is woefully limited. Why even bother with God? Doesn't God have to regularly intervene to protect us from harm in order to be worth our attention at all?*

But what if the defining quality of what we call God is something more profound than active omnipotence? What if the arbitrary and micromanaging God sometimes taught in Sunday School was the result of an earlier phase in the evolution of human thought, spirituality, and ethical awareness? Perhaps from a contemporary perspective God the All-Powerful is actually too small, too *limited* a God. Is it possible to conceive the divine dimension of reality in a more subtle way?

We can see why tribes and cultures in the past would want to believe in a caretaker God, a heavenly judge and guardian. After all, the belief that if you avoid causing evil, no evil will befall you, is very comforting. The trouble is, it doesn't seem to be true. Bible-believing Christians and Qur'an-following Muslims are no less likely to die in random traffic accidents or rockslides or floods than anyone else. Jews, of course, have known for millennia that their existence on this planet is precarious. Experience taught them early that it was not the daily business of the Almighty to guarantee even the most righteous their safety and prosperity, much less to protect them from every hand raised to harm them.

A God Who Is Present Everywhere

A little reflection suggests more adequate ways of conceiving and relating to God. For example, if God exists, wouldn't it make more sense that people would access God through established science, reason, core religious and ethical principles, and philosophy, rather than through miraculous signs and wonders that compel belief? Wouldn't it be fitting for men and women to respond to a "God of Love" with their questions, doubts, and deep reflections, rather than dismissing doubts and questions as sinful? Faith and spirituality need not require the abdication of reason and a regression to a more childlike, authority-based way of thinking.

What if we replaced omnipotence with omnipresence as the defining attribute of what we understand as God? If the big G in God connotes unlimited power, let's try using a lowercase g instead, so as to distinguish more clearly between the two different conceptions of the divine. The god of love gives rise to the sense of an omnipresence that connects us all, and a reverence for the deep interconnectedness that calls us to the path of love and the common good. This awareness that we are all interconnected is pivotal for dealing with global problems. As Dr. Martin Luther King Jr. put it in his famous Christmas sermon of December 24, 1967, "Peace on Earth":

> It really boils down to this: that all life is interrelated. We are all caught in an inescapable network of mutuality, tied into a single garment of destiny. Whatever affects one directly, affects all indirectly.[24]

The more people who experience and live this way of being, the better off the world will be.

Is it even reasonable, however, to believe that there may be some kind of draw toward love and goodness at the core of the universe? If the major monotheistic religions were wrong about omnipotence, might they be wrong about omnibenevolence as well?

Omnibenevolence: "Perfect and Unchanging," or "Good"?

To the biblical picture of God, the classical Christian theologians such as Thomas Aquinas added the ancient Greek contention, affirmed by both Plato and Aristotle, that the divine must also be "unchanging." After all, if God is perfect, all-powerful, and all-knowing, God must never change, since change would imply that God had not been quite perfect to begin with.

Classical theologians also assumed that this perfect, unchanging God would not feel emotions such as grief or regret. These emotions are responses to events in the world; but if God responds to anything, then God changes, and what is perfect cannot change. Moreover, grief and regret (it was said) could not be felt by an all-powerful, all-knowing, unchanging, perfect being, for these emotions represent a state that is inferior to perfect contentment.

It is difficult to imagine an empathetic relationship—indeed, *any* real relationship—with this kind of God. To many today, it seems odd that such a nonrelational view of God would have a significant impact on Judaism, Christianity, and Islam. After all, the Hebrew Bible, which deeply influenced all three traditions, portrays a volatile God who engages in a compassionate relationship with his people, experiences "negative" emotions such as anger or grief at their bad decisions, and even changes his mind on occasion.

A "Lure" toward Good

We have already pointed out that the evidence science provides about natural processes is completely compatible with the idea of a dynamic divinity that is present in the relational life force, energy, and creativity that are clearly visible on our planet, and elsewhere in the universe as well. Furthermore, we have already discovered that these natural processes could be said to provide a lure or trend toward goodness, beauty, and wonder that is intrinsic to our interconnected cosmos. If you're fuzzy on how this could be possible, pause here to reread the existential summaries at the end of the previous science sections: Cosmology and Astrophysics in Chapter 3, Biology and Evolution in Chapter 4 (remember "survival of the most cooperative"?), and Neuroscience in Chapter 5. Goodness fits well with omnipresence as a divine attribute, as long as omnipotence isn't in the mix.

God as an unchanging "perfect" entity, however, is very difficult to reconcile with a never-finished, constantly changing creation. So we encourage you to seriously question "perfect" and "unchanging" as viable descriptions of god. The basic creative *nature* of the divine force does not change, but god's *experience* of creation is constantly changing, in continual response to its creatures' decisions and actions. We are always readjusting to the ever-new present that each of us co-creates, based on our own choices, on choices of other humans, on our interactions with other species, and on the forces of nature.

Omniscience: Are Our Futures Predetermined?

Omniscience, the knowledge of everything, is another of the major attributes of God in traditional Jewish, Christian, and Muslim belief, and is closely related to omnipotence. If God can do all, and has done all, God must know all—not only all that has been and is now, but also all that will be: the future.

But, like the idea of an omnipotent God, the concept of an omniscient God poses many ethical as well as rational problems.

If God knows the future, the future, it would seem, must be predetermined, which would mean that freedom is an illusion. The ancient theologian Saint Augustine imagined every moment of time laid out before God like a great landscape, a panorama of which God sees every detail. To mere mortals, things seem to happen in time, moment by moment, as if time were real and our actions influenced our future. But because God beholds all time simultaneously, with nothing hidden from God's sight, clearly there is no future as mortals understand it. Though time seems to "pass" and events seem to "happen," in fact all events already, unchangeably, exist.

This is not the universe that science knows today. In the previous chapters on science and nature, we described how the past constrains what can happen in possible futures. Within those constraints, however, there are numerous outcomes in which randomness rules. And because all of creation is interrelated, many things influence which among various possible outcomes actually comes about. Depending on a vast array of contingencies, including what we and the rest of the universe do next, a very different future may arise. A uranium atom may or may not decay; a mutation may or may not arise in an animal fetus; the president may or may not push the red button that starts a nuclear war. You may or may not be on the beach when an unexpected tsunami hits the country where you are vacationing. So, the future is constantly in process, becoming new and different every split second, based on a huge collection of contingent factors.

To assign God complete knowledge of the future raises scientific, theological, and ethical problems. The ethical problem is *fatalism*. If the future is predetermined, then theoretically you can do whatever you like and it won't matter. Such a level of divine control takes away the incentive to work for a better future, because *qué será, será*—whatever will be, will be. As we noted in the previous chapter, psychologists have conducted experiments that show that reducing a person's belief in free will makes that person more likely to act selfishly and aggressively, rather than empathetically and cooperatively. So the way your belief system interprets God's omniscience can deeply affect your sense of personal responsibility.

An Omnipresent God

If God knows all human "choices" in advance, it must be that in some sense they already exist to be known. The best explanation for why they already exist would be a timeless God. And if that is true, then we actually do not choose our beliefs or words or actions.

Imagine that you are preparing for a college examination. Now imagine that, before the creation of the world, God already knew about this examination—and whether or not you would pass it. Then your success, it would seem, does not depend on your own free agency; you cannot affect an outcome predestined for all time. And if that is so, does it really matter if you spend the night before the test partying instead of studying?

The early Protestant theologian John Calvin took divine omniscience to its logical conclusion: If God knows everything, God knows who will be saved and who will be damned, because *God is the One* who predestined each human being to salvation or to eternal torment in hell. All you can do is follow God as if you were saved and hope that you actually are. But you can't really change the outcome. Though you hold the correct beliefs and perform the right actions all your life, if you are predestined for hell, you will experience a loss of faith on your deathbed, or something else will happen that will damn you. You are powerless to alter this outcome. A God who would create such a system seems capricious and tyrannical, rather than a God of infinite love and goodness.

Present in All Our Possible Futures

But there is another concept of divine knowing that raises fewer theological and scientific problems. It is the belief that the omnipresent god retains the memory of all past events, is fully present with creatures at each moment of time, and in some sense attracts us toward choosing positive actions, yet without determining the outcome. On this view, omnipresence is the key divine attribute. If this god is truly present everywhere, the divine experience encompasses all of our pasts and presents. God also knows our *potential* futures in each moment. But not even a personified omnipresence can know the outcome of a free decision until it happens—there are just too many contingencies.

And for readers who are sci-fi buffs: Okay. *Perhaps* at some point in the distant future, our transhuman descendants may figure out how to "time travel" by way of other dimensions. If that's even possible, we'd expect that the science fiction authors who have imagined this scenario got it right: If something or someone could make a change in the past, it would change the future, which would be our present. So far, that doesn't seem to have happened, but we'll never know for sure. And if it did, that still doesn't make the future predetermined.

* * *

Let us close this chapter by pulling together all the issues we've raised concerning the traditional picture of God. As soon as we begin to step outside that still-dominant framework for thinking about divinity, more attractive ways of imagining god begin to emerge. Then we can consider the powerful ways these new understandings of god can help us interpret the world and inspire our actions in it.

The "Almighty Father" Version of God No Longer Works, If It Ever Did . . .

When you get right down to it, if God is all-powerful, perfect, and unchanging, and knows the future, then this *must* be "the best of all possible worlds." Such a God—we'll call him the "Almighty Father"—would have had the foreknowledge to make it so. His perfect nature would have required him to make it so, and his omnipotence would have guaranteed that he did. So if this is not the best possible world, then either God failed in his object (which he cannot do, given his perfect nature), or else he does not exist.

Candide and Dr. Pangloss

One of the most entertaining novellas to come out of the Enlightenment, Voltaire's *Candide* (1759), examines this question with devastating wit. In a picaresque series of adventures, Voltaire has the young Candide experience some of the horrors and injustices of this "best of all possible worlds," as his philosophy tutor Dr. Pangloss describes it. In spite of Candide's skepticism, Pangloss continues to insist on this description even after the good doctor barely survives a murder attempt and then is sold into slavery.

Imagine that an omnipotent, omniscient, and perfectly good God purposely created this world with the knowledge that millions of innocent children would suffer and die; that genocides, human trafficking, torture, rape, plagues, and wars would be commonplace; and that a hell of endless torment would be necessary to eternally house not only those who caused all this evil and misery, but also those who may have done good works in life, but failed to worship God under the right name or hold the right beliefs concerning his nature.

It is hard to think of such a God as the best of all possible Gods, let alone as a perfect one.

When we read *Candide*, we can't help being fond of Dr. Pangloss, loopy as he is. He reminds of us of those well-meaning theologians and church leaders who insist on the omnipotent "Almighty Father" version of God, rather than acknowledging that the world they live in does not support it. Instead, they proclaim, "It is a mystery beyond human comprehension," for "Who can understand the infinite mind of God?" We feel that these responses are just not enough.

Goodness versus "Might Makes Right"

A number of the Old Testament writers believed in the "Almighty Father" concept of God, who was all-good *because* he was all-powerful: Eternal Might made Eternal Right. Although patriarchs and prophets like Abraham and Moses were allowed to question God, they were not allowed to dispute his answers.

If you believed that God wanted you to sacrifice the firstlings of your flock, or even your firstborn child, you did that. If you believed that God wanted your people to be tortured and sold into slavery because you hadn't provided adequate burnt offerings or had occasionally worshiped other gods, you accepted God's judgment and its consequences.

Thus did the ancient writers explain—and at the same time dignify—the misfortunes of the small, vulnerable community to which they belonged. The real reason their people were conquered and oppressed was undoubtedly because they were a relatively powerless minority living in a hotly contested crossroads of land and sea between two major, militarily brutal empires—not because they were obstinate children deserving an Almighty Father's chastisement.

The "Almighty Father" version of God was carried fairly intact into Christianity, even though leading Jewish rabbis had begun questioning its adequacy before Jesus was born. The dominance of this one model is puzzling when you look at Jesus's teachings and actions, which offered a different concept of the one he called "Abba" or "Father"—one that, like the evolving rabbinical teachings of the time, included the possibility of greater human autonomy, dignity, and moral progress.

It was the Roman Emperor Constantine who worked to restore the Almighty God to supremacy, some three centuries after Jesus's death. Constantine made Christianity the imperial religion, and used it to justify the expansion of his empire and legitimize the political and cultural establishment it represented.

The Christian version of the "Almighty Father" is the earthly emperor glorified: the attributes of Caesar reimagined as the attributes of God. He holds unquestionable, absolute power. He demands unquestioning obedience and casts out, punishes, or destroys those who question or fail to obey him. He presides over a hierarchy that extends his authority more directly to his followers. His word is infallible: If he contradicts a known truth, you must reject that truth. If he says that something wrong is right, such as a law that oppresses people, you accept it, even if, internally, you know it is wrong. Doubting God's word is a sin, just as doubting Caesar's is a crime.

This picture of God, we contend, cannot be "good" for thinking adults. The human father who wants absolute control of his children, who prevents them from maturing and attaining independence, is rightly considered abusive, and often those who were raised with such an image of God find it difficult to love him as the Bible commands. Not surprisingly, many people today are no longer comfortable with this might-makes-right definition of goodness. That isn't goodness as we know it.

Is It Really Such a Crazy System?

Basically, things are set up so that human beings take care of each other and the world, whether you believe that God, god, or natural events caused things to be this way. In all our flawed, imperfect glory, we're the ones who make our families, our communities, our countries, and our planet either places of grace or living hells—or, more usually, something in between the two.

Both science and history make it clear that we (and in a sense, everything in the universe) have been co-creators with god. Out of future possibilities, and within the constraints imposed by the past, we generate the present. Some of us (including one of this book's authors) believe that we co-create with the divine lure. But both authors believe that God does not do the work for us, nor does a coercive divine power impose the outcome.

An Omnipresent God

Clearly, there will always be those who believe in an all-powerful, perfect, future-knowing God. We are making the case that this traditional picture of God is not the only possible one. For many thinking people it just doesn't work, morally or realistically. Neither does it express the understanding of the divine that is most likely to enlighten and unite the world and lead it to justice and peace.

If you are a girl raised in a well-off Los Angeles neighborhood, you will have many more plentiful and promising future possibilities than a girl raised in a poor village controlled by the Taliban in the Swat District of Pakistan. Likewise, if you are a monarch butterfly migrating today, you will have different, much more limited future possibilities than your more plentiful ancestors, now that much of the butterfly-friendly habitat along your 2,500-mile migration route has been destroyed.

There doesn't seem to be a God who is magically intervening to change these girls' or these butterflies' outcomes. Rather, all of us are being called to work for positive changes, when and where we are in a position to do so—if only we heed the call.

None of us is perfect; humans do not always do what's right, or come through challenges consistently well. Sometimes we allow, even cause, unspeakably awful things to happen.

But when you experience a completely unexpected act of kindness at a hard time in your life, or witness a community coming together to restore a river or a habitat that previous human activity has made a wasteland, or see a previously heedless society beginning to look out for its poor, its ill, and its disadvantaged members, you realize that humans really do have the divine ability to reduce suffering and bring about good in the world. And if you think that this whole process has something to do with god, you may be right.

We need space for a more mature, accountable, and reflective spirituality. We need a religion that has come of age for a humanity that has come of age, with a god that is credible for the dilemmas of the twenty-first century. There is plenty in what we now know to be true about nature and the cosmos that suggests other, more viable pictures of what ultimate omnipresent goodness (whether divine or natural) might look like. In the next chapter we examine some of the most promising pictures.

7

Religion Comes of Age

MANY PEOPLE TAKE GREAT comfort in the belief that God is good, that God planned creation with us in mind, that we are the pinnacle of God's creation, and that God knows and loves us. These beliefs, often the subject of sermons, are familiar and heartwarming. But which of them can be validated from the evidence of science and nature?

The answer is ambiguous. As we have said, love is as much a basic necessity for individuals as cooperation is for societies. The science of ecology teaches that all living things evolve toward optimal interrelations within their environment—a sort of natural harmony. It is certainly not a stretch to believe that the ground of all being—which so many call God—pulls toward a harmony of the cosmos, which we call love. Presumably a loving god is also a good god. By contrast, when you factor in all the evidence of nature and science, the belief that God is an Almighty Father who originally created the universe with humans in mind and knew exactly what was going to happen to them in advance—well, that's a bit more of a stretch.

The issue here is the divine distance. Throughout history, some theologians have stressed divine transcendence to such an extent that they've had trouble making sense of a God who is really present with, and concerned about, the individual beings in creation. Others have made large claims on behalf of a providential God who helps humans and personally intervenes in the world—claims that run aground on the rocks of scientific objections or narrative inconsistencies of their own. Both groups of thinkers, whatever their intentions, leave us with God as an "outside being." The unapproachability, or rather absence, of this God grew so apparent in the modern age that critics began to call him "*Deus absconditus*"—the God who has absconded, disappeared.

It is tempting to poke fun at the outside God, the one who has grown so transcendent as to no longer play any role in the world. Why would such a God create the universe in the first place—out of curiosity, out of boredom, or perhaps for a lark, to see what would happen?[25] Does this distant God really care about us motley humans? If a random asteroid happened to destroy us, God might miss *The Human Show*, but would God then wait dispassionately to see whether another intelligent species evolved to fill our niche? Also, it is hard to see how a distant God who is never really present with creation at all could be "good" in any sense that we understand.

A Good God for Our Times

There is, however, a *nonoutside* concept of God, the one we have been calling god, that fits much better with science, nature, and goodness. For both theists and skeptics, this can be described as "the sacred" or "the divine," with additional words for theists such as "indwelling" and "all-pervading."

It is not a stretch to say this all-pervading god is good. After all, interrelatedness is at the core of the universe; it calls us to practice love and compassion—deeply religious ideals—in order to sustain it. Even the morally neutral biological phenomenon of evolution rewards cooperation. Over the eons, cooperation has been taking organisms and ecosystems in a direction of greater complexity and beauty. Furthermore, humanity's cultural evolution seems to be taking us (in fits and starts) in a direction of greater interconnection, oneness, and awareness of our interdependence. In other words, evolution seems to have an aspirational quality on both the biological and cultural levels.

For theists, *the concept of god expresses the value dimension in all that is*. Each thing has its own value, makes its unique contribution to the whole. And god is what we understand to be the ground and source of all that goodness. So, the concept of the divine not only is good, but it also continually calls us to goodness; it asks us to transcend primitive biological drives and tap into the evolutionary gifts of higher intelligence, cooperation, and love, in order to co-create a better future for ourselves and our planet.

PART TWO: RELIGION COMES OF AGE

The Ultimate Mystery

Viewed in this way, god is the ultimate mystery, before which we stand in silence and awe. Many of us with a religious background or beliefs have experienced this transcendence at certain times in our lives. Those of us who are atheists or agnostics have experienced such moments as well. These are the experiences that inspire all of us to embrace goodness at its best.

Think about them: the moments when we are conscious of the raw sheer givenness, grandeur, and mystery of the cosmos. The moment when addicts give up control of their lives to something ineffable, something they can't describe, and suddenly their addiction loses its grip. The moment when a transcendent love and compassion for all of those around us, even for creation itself, overwhelms us, so that we act in caring and selfless ways.

This thing that gives meaning, that serves as the ground for all good, that motivates us to live with compassion, that lifts us beyond ourselves—this we call the sacred. The source of goodness has to be as complex as all the complexity in the universe. It doesn't explain everything, nor does it preprogram everything from the outset. But in some sense it *does* serve as the goal for all things.

What kind of communion can we have with the sacred?

Our ancestors' concepts of god may have been problematic, but they still knew how to commune with the sacred. In many ways, their practices still work; they represent the responses humans have always had when they experience the ineffable.

We mentioned some of them earlier—meditation, living ethically, studying creation, exploring theology. To these we can add silence; centering; community; taking steps to conserve our ecosystem for future generations; working for peace and justice; taking the side of the poor and oppressed; becoming conscious of the sacred in our fellow humans, in nature, in music, in a great novel, or in art. Taken together, these practices are vastly more attractive than the options for reaching the "outside" God.

Your Religious or Nonreligious Heritage Is a Starting Point

Communing with the ultimate in this way also produces and nurtures a deep humility. It means admitting that no one religion holds a monopoly on all truth, and that the best path to the sacred will vary from person to person, depending on each one's temperament, culture, and the religious or nonreligious practices that lead each of them to their deepest spiritual encounters. Any religious heritage can serve as an open and humble starting point for a person's spiritual quest. In fact, as long as established science is accepted (and that's a big if), the world might be better off if religions were introduced in this more open way in the churches, temples, and mosques where people follow a particular faith.

Finding this something that is both all-pervading and transcendent, that draws us all toward the good, is a lifelong process. It offers countless moments of enlightenment along the way.

Yet, to be intellectually honest, no one can give *the* definitive definition of the all-pervading, transcendent sacred. The god that fits in a box is not god. Rather, the most we can offer is a framework for talking about the sacred, leaving it to you to fill in the specifics of your understanding of and relationship to the ultimate in the ways that you believe communicate it the best. Of course, all of us can learn from each other along the way, from the great spiritual teachers of the past, and from the teachers of our day. We might sometimes wish that a single path, a single set of beliefs, could serve as the authoritative guide for all people. But the plurality of cultures, historical periods, and places that gave rise to our religions goes against the dream of One Authority, One Answer.

Yes, we can attempt to live life from and toward the sacred. But no one can hand you the sacred on a platter.

Open-Ended, Inviting Ways of Talking About the Sacred

Religion, science, and philosophy have given us numerous ways to talk about ultimacies and the process of creation. The following concepts are not dogma; they are simply guides, frameworks, and invitations to thought and action. Without depending on a specific narrative or symbolism, they embrace and enable the spirit of awe, love, and moral obligation found in all of humanity and in the best of our faith traditions.

The first three concepts assume there is something divine at the root of everything; they work well for people of faith:

- Omnipresence: God is present everywhere.
- Divine Indwelling: We and all of creation are permeated by the divine presence; we dwell within divinity; we share in what it is to be divine.

- Panentheism (pan-en-theism): the divine is in all things, *and* all things are somehow within the all-encompassing divine presence (This is more than simply pantheism, which holds that everything that exists is divine, that all things are god or are parts of god).[26]

These next three concepts neither require nor exclude a divine being:

- Naturalism and science: There is a natural order, which exists and operates without miraculous interventions by a supernatural being.
- Aesthetics: Beauty exists, and can be appreciated, including the incredible beauty of the cosmos. Physicists often exclaim about the elegance of the equations that describe the universe. In fact, if an equation is not elegant, they contend, it likely will turn out to be false.
- Creativity: Biologists, on the other hand, ask us to appreciate the creative variety, novelty, complexity, and intimacy of life in nature.

Where Morality and Ethics Fit In

Throughout history, ethics and morality have continually changed as humans gained more insight into their own nature and the nature of the world around them. The severe and sometimes arbitrary rulings attributed to God in Leviticus, for example, reflect the Bronze Age worldview of the writers of that book. A completely literal adherence to the exact prescriptions of that ethical system would have more in common with the values of the Taliban, who cling to a similar ancient and insular mindset, than they do with our values today.

Certainly ethics and morality should inform our discussion of god. After all, if the idea of god did not positively affect how we live in the world, it would not be worth having. But the reality is that the religious dogmas people cling to often make it more difficult, not easier, to follow the great core values of goodness, love, compassion, justice, and connectedness. They can hold us back from new ethical insights that are gained as our species continues to evolve.

If we are going to survive together on this planet, embracing an ever-deeper understanding of what love and compassion require really matters. For example, the best way of judging a value in our modern world might be by considering how well it connects us to the rest of creation in a positive way—how close it brings us to understanding, acceptance, kinship, and love of all the different kinds of humans and other creatures in the world.

What's beautiful about this approach to god and ethics is that it opens up a way of speaking about god

- that credits humanity with a full capacity for ethical and spiritual reasoning;
- that doesn't require suppressing the intellect;
- that isn't demeaning to any fellow human of any race, religion, nationality, ethnic group, or gender;
- that resonates with our deepest ethical intuitions;
- that draws on the human need to locate ourselves within a bigger story;
- that is inspired by and consistent with science and reality;
- that draws people together rather than separating them,
- that affirms altruism rather than tribalism;
- and that supports the preservation of the earth, its health, and its resources.

Religion has always been about a right relationship with god, each other, and the world. The pre-scientific worldviews of early adherents to the world's religions sometimes gave them harsh (and to us, unethical) ideas about what these right relationships required. Our species has learned a great deal since then. Incredible advances in both scientific knowledge and moral understanding have been made, and much has changed.

Humanity is finally beginning to realize that we don't live in a static universe with an unchanging King in charge. Rather, we live in a world of constant movement and creative becoming—from the inward depths of subatomic energy, up through earthly creatures' consciousnesses, and out into the most spectacular phenomena of our cosmos.

This new sense of existence offers exciting possibilities for participating in, and co-forming, the future of our world. The processes that have created and continue to create through the systems of interconnected energy and evolution offer a way of conceiving the sacred that resonates deeply with the dynamically changing earth as we have come to know it. Humanity is beginning to conceive a co-creator that not only lives in the beauty of nature and the stillness of the present moment, but also in the open-ended evolutionary processes and in the myriad of possible becomings that beckon to us from the future.

We are convinced that spiritually grounded worldviews based on scientific realities will facilitate ever more constructive ways to move forward as we face the challenges and opportunities generated by the approximately 8 billion humans who currently live on Earth. No longer will we believe god's role is just to liberate our souls from the world, but rather to make us part of the great work of renewing and healing the earth and everything it contains.

Constructive Redefinitions of God, Religion, and Faith

To put it another way, we are free to conceive god with ever-increasing insight as science and culture evolve. Some revere god as a not-less-than-personal ultimate reality; others imagine god as the personification of the energy and creativity that animates all of creation, the indwelling and transcendent energy that draws all of us toward wholeness. Both are inspired by an awe and wonder toward that which is beyond comprehension.

How might this reverence express itself in action?

Think of the saints of our time: Gandhi, Dorothy Day, the Dalai Lama, Martin Luther King Jr., Desmond Tutu, Jane Goodall, Malala Yusufzai... Each of them exhibits an inspiring spirit of bravery, commitment to justice, a concern for the oppressed, and a bias toward action. And each of them has made the world a better place. Their actions are clearly motivated by something beyond the narrow love for family and tribe.

And it is not just saintlike people who demonstrate that higher degree of compassion that we call love. Every person can be an influence for good within their areas of work and expertise—occasionally, if they are fortunate, in a major way. Surely their actions transcend biologically based love, pointing to a spiritual energy that works through anyone and everyone who is open to its draw, even when the opening is the tiniest of slits. It is for this reason that we agree with the faith traditions when they proclaim, "God is Love."

Religion and the Sacred
An Existential Summary of Chapter 7

WE PAUSE HERE TO summarize what insight the above concepts of the sacred and religion can give us into the questions of our existence:

- The science chapters (3–5) recounted how everything in the cosmos is interconnected, from the grandest galaxy to the most annoying parasite to the almost-impossible-to-detect Higgs boson ("the God particle"). Furthermore, everything in the cosmos is constantly in process: emerging, evolving, ever-changing. We humans, in fact, only emerged relatively recently in cosmic history.
- In this chapter and the preceding one (6–7) we united that evidence with concepts of goodness. We explored what, if anything, the realities of the cosmos might tell us about how traditional beliefs about God and religion stack up with the realities of science in addressing the basic questions of our existence. We concluded that some traditional beliefs seem to fit well with nature. For example, god could certainly be said to be omnipresent. But other beliefs just don't seem to work with the science and ethics of our day, such as the common belief that there's an almighty God who intervenes supernaturally in human affairs. A good God and an all-powerful God appear to be mutually exclusive. If a god does exist, the evidence seems to suggest, it must be one that is growing and adapting along with us and the rest of creation.

- We also offered evidence to support the many faith traditions that proclaim, "God is Love." They are describing the omnipresent (divine) lure that is responsible not only for our creativity and attraction to beauty, but also for the inner voice that calls us to care for ourselves, our loved ones, our community, and the wider world, including those we think of as "other." Based on the nature of this call, we suggested correspondingly new definitions for religion and faith.

- Religion is no longer about fixed answers; it is about discovery and awe. That means the quest for scientific discoveries is part and parcel of the spiritual quest of our age, because science is always on the cutting edge of the ongoing pursuit of new understanding. Furthermore, religion for an evolving humanity cannot be about supporting an exclusive tribe of believers, but rather about joining an open community of seekers. In our estimation, scientists dedicated to the pursuit of truth are, in an important sense, a part of the spiritual quest—even those who would not call themselves religious.

- Likewise, faith is no longer a matter of mandatory creeds or precise definitions of god. Rather it is a trust that in some sense love is at the heart of the universe, that this Love is ultimately more powerful than violence and selfishness, and that it infuses all of us in discernible and indiscernible ways, constantly calling us to wholeness and connection.

- This omnipresent energy or spirit is whatever draws us and the ever-emerging cosmic creation toward beauty, diversity, creativity, connectivity, consciousness, goodness, wisdom, and awe. Whether we call it god or not, it is a wonderful feeling to awaken to this spiritual connection with all that is wonderful in the universe.

- How do we orient ourselves toward this spiritual connection? Each of the things we consider sacred—the things that drive, inspire, and motivate us (family, ethics, environment, community, social justice, beauty, and many others)—also tend to be the things that help us rise above our singular, isolated self. They point to the greater good in multiple ways, whether it is understood as transcendence or emergence or creativity or all-connectedness. And it is this animating desire that we might call good, god, or simply sacred.

8

A Way to Hold Both Your Faith and Your Doubts

THE PREVIOUS CHAPTERS SUGGESTED new ways of looking at our existence, at religion, and at god that conform to realities we now know to be true, realities that call into question some cherished and long-held traditional beliefs. For that reason, devout readers from traditional faith backgrounds may find them seriously unsettling (including our religious friends who were kind enough to read prepublished drafts of this book and give comments). So we'd like to pause here and address that issue.

Questioning Used to Get You Killed

As science has advanced and pluralism has become more common, various polls have shown that even Americans, the most religious of the Westerners, are now much more likely to question, change, or leave their religion than they were in past generations. A March 2021 Gallup poll found, for the first time in recent history, that fewer than 50 percent of Americans were members of a church, synagogue, or mosque. And the numbers continue to drop.[27]

We are fortunate to live in an era in which we're allowed to openly question. This freedom is a relatively recent phenomenon in human history. In earlier centuries—and in some parts of the world today—people could be severely punished, even executed, for publicly questioning their faith.

During the time of the Roman Empire, it was widely believed that the earth was the center of the universe. So heaven must be in the sky, somewhere above the stars, and hell must be below the earth (which was, of course, flat). Since these beliefs represented the best observations and knowledge available to the scholars in southern Europe at the time, they were presupposed by the early Christian authors as they wrote, and eventually became a part of the sacred writings known as the New Testament. Once the Bible became the official holy book of Christendom, its scientific errors were enshrined as religious beliefs, and questioning them became dangerous.

Thus began a long history of the church's resistance to new scientific knowledge that extends even into the present. In the 1500s, when Copernicus concluded that the sun rather than the earth was the center of our universe, he waited until just before he died to publish his discovery, and so escaped prosecution. Giordano Bruno was not so fortunate. In 1600, he was burned at the stake for supporting the findings of Copernicus, and for proposing that our solar system might be just one of a large number of similar systems. (Actually, what sealed his fate was his claim that multiple worlds meant multiple Christs must have come, one to save the people of each planet; this got him convicted of heresy.) When Galileo later championed astronomical discoveries that contradicted church doctrine, he, too, was condemned as a heretic. In 1633 he was forced to recant his findings, and he spent the rest of his life under house arrest.

Contradicting one's religion can still mean death or imprisonment if you live in a theocracy. But otherwise, heresy prosecutions are no longer common. That is not to say there are no penalties for questioners. Some of the more conservative religious communities may ostracize those who no longer hold the correct beliefs, or continually pressure them to "come back to the faith." In fact, conservative religious leaders often discourage their followers from questioning, because they believe it is a sin to challenge what they believe to be God's Word.

Acknowledging Doubts Helps You Grow

We strongly disagree. In the first place, given all the contradictory religious claims, it is highly unlikely that any particular faith has a monopoly on the absolute truth about God. On a more general level, suppressing questions stifles creative thinking, hurts scientific inquiry, and often causes the questioners' doubts to increase rather than diminish.

Defining doubts as sin raises the guilt level, but it rarely helps people to work through their doubts. Questioning may indeed lead to changes in your understanding of God and your beliefs about the world, but you will have a deeper, more meaningful faith if you seek answers to your questions instead of trying to bury them.

Finally, questioning could even save your life. Think of the unquestioning cult members who have followed their leaders into great danger, even mass suicide.

For believers, however, especially those from families or cultures where questioning is forbidden, it can be an alarming and gut-wrenching dilemma.

When believers who grow up inside a cocoon of faith are gradually exposed to a more diverse culture, they meet others who have different belief systems. This frequently causes them to question some of their own beliefs. Often they feel disloyal for harboring such doubts. If they have been taught that it is wrong to question, they may feel so guilty that they try to suppress the growing suspicion that certain aspects of their faith are problematic. Or they may question the inherited claims of their tradition up to a certain point and then stop abruptly, afraid they might conclude that beliefs they and their families have cherished are wrong.

Even if they stay safely within the tightly knit community of their own religious schools, services, and social gatherings, what they hear of modern science may still cause doubts, especially if they have been taught that their ancient sacred texts must be taken as literal truth.

Prominent antireligion atheists have received plenty of media attention for their claims that science, and in particular evolution, proves there is no God. This causes believers to wonder if they, too, must be antiscience in order to remain faithful. It puts such believers in the untenable position of denying verifiable truths in the name of the God of Truth.

Atheists Have Doubts, Too

It is not just believers who are reluctant to acknowledge their doubts. Atheists may be embarrassed by occasional yearnings for a faith they consider anti-intellectual, one that members of their own circle would not accept. Both atheists and people of faith may wonder why they believe a particular doctrine some of the time and doubt it at other times.

Part Two: Religion Comes of Age

It is, however, human nature to doubt. In fact, if you feel guilty about your doubts and questions because you believe God will punish you for seeking the truth, we would like to gently suggest that you, of all people, most definitely should be reexamining your concept of God. And a useful and even comforting way to do that is "The Percentage Exercise."

The Percentage Exercise

In chapter 7 of their book *The Predicament of Belief: Science, Philosophy, Faith*, Philip Clayton, coauthor of this book, and Steven Knapp came up with a helpful way of holding your beliefs and doubts as you assess them. They used more academic language, but basically the concept works like this:

You assign a rough percentage to the likelihood of each belief or doubt being true, even if you do so with wild guesses at first. For this process, your estimates can be based on personal experiences and emotions as well as intellectual reasoning.

Here are some actual examples of how it works, based on people we know (because of privacy issues, we have changed their names and some of their life details). The people in each of these examples—Sarah, Matthew, and Meryem—could have just given up and suppressed their doubts, because of the conflicting pull between those doubts and their beliefs. They each found it more helpful to acknowledge both doubts and beliefs, to seek to understand and evaluate them, and to begin looking for answers they could live with—even if these answers would inevitably change over time.

- Sarah was raised in a nonreligious family and is now a biologist who considers herself a rational atheist. When she reads about the latest discoveries in quantum physics, however, those awe-inspiring revelations combined with the experiences she is having as a new mother make her wonder if there might be some kind of a god after all. She doesn't think there is, but she realizes the idea is attractive to her. So she decides to begin to investigate the possibility of god's existence more thoroughly.

    Sarah may say that right now she is about 60 percent sure that there is no god, but that it is not something she's investigated very thoroughly. So she plans to embark on an investigation.

    Let's say that two years from now, Sarah's investigation has convinced her that both the arguments and her personal experience favor

A Way to Hold Both Your Faith and Your Doubts

the existence of what she thinks of as "Something More." At that time, she may decide she's now (say) 60 percent certain that some kind of god exists, thus acknowledging that she still has doubts. Given that she's at this place, she feels comfortable in the new relationship she has developed with her concept of god and enjoys occasionally attending the open-minded local church that she and her family have joined. She thinks it is highly unlikely that most of the church's supernatural doctrines are literally true. However, she finds that considering these doctrines metaphorically inspires her to live more thoughtfully. She also enjoys helping with the church's food bank with her young daughter, because it gives her a concrete way to serve others in their community, and is a good experience for both of them.

Since Sarah is a seeker, she may go back and forth between 60 percent no-supernatural-god and 60 percent no-god-at-all for the rest of her life, depending on circumstances and subsequent new knowledge she acquires. She even jokes that whether or not she believes in god depends on what day of the week it is. Because she has acknowledged that it is not a provable either/or proposition, however, she's comfortable with both her doubts and beliefs.

- Matthew, on the other hand, has been raised a Christian and used to accept the basic beliefs he was taught. Those beliefs have changed over time, however, and now they tend more toward a nonsupernatural god rather than the Almighty Father of his tradition. He also has trouble believing in the literal miracles of Jesus, including a literal resurrection. Matthew has concluded that the resurrection of Jesus is a valuable metaphor for many spiritual truths he holds dear.

    However, his relationship with his wife is quite rocky at this time, and he wonders if part of the problem is somehow related to his traditional religious upbringing and philosophical views.

    Matthew may say that right now he is about 98 percent sure there is a god, but also fairly certain—say, 80 percent—that the miracles and resurrection of Jesus are not literally true. That doesn't hurt his faith as a Christian, however. He still finds comfort and inspiration in his spiritual life in the Christian tradition; he enjoys attending his church and participating in church efforts to be "the hands and feet of Jesus" in the world.

    One thing Matthew freely admits: At the height of his church's beautiful annual Easter celebration, and despite his usual skepticism, that percentage changes: he feels as though "Christ is risen indeed!" Moved by the music and the messages, he imagines the stone rolled away from the tomb and being a witness as the angels proclaim that Jesus lives. At that moment, even though he is tacitly aware that he doesn't really believe it literally, he finds himself believing. Like moments of being caught up in the world of a great opera or play, he decides to let these moments of literal belief stand. They are immensely meaningful to him, and he has found a way to incorporate them into his life, even though they don't represent his settled opinion.

He is still completely in the dark about his marital problems, though, as well as about what part his religious beliefs may or may not play in this area of his life. So he chooses to avoid thinking about or dealing with those issues for now.

- Meryem was raised in a loving, highly educated Muslim family in Istanbul, and has always believed Islam is the one true religion without even thinking about it, since everyone she knew there was Muslim. Ever since her teen years, she has thought of much of the Qur'an as allegorical, so she isn't bothered by some of its suras (chapters) that seem to contradict science. Now she is a student at USC in California, and is getting many questions about her religion from new friends in her classes, her dorm, and at interfaith events she attends through the campus Muslim group she has joined. Although she admits it to no one, she is experiencing many internal questions about her faith, and wondering if such thoughts are betraying her family and putting her soul at risk.

  Meryem decides that she is (as she puts it) 99.9 percent sure that God is a God of truth and love as well as judgment. God will understand and accept her questions, she says, since they are genuine concerns that she is struggling with. (She doesn't mention them to her family, however). She decides she is 95 percent sure that Islam is the one true faith, though she recognizes that her assurance might change as she explores her beliefs further during her time at USC.

  Then Meryem finds out that research shows that education in an interreligious context actually deepens a person's understanding of his or her own tradition more effectively than monoreligious education. So she relaxes and enjoys her interfaith interactions. By the time she graduates, she admits (internally) that she is now only about 75 percent sure that Islam is the one true faith. Although it might seem

A Way to Hold Both Your Faith and Your Doubts

paradoxical to others, she now considers herself a much better Muslim with a much deeper faith in God. She also feels better equipped to work with those from other faiths for the common good.

* * *

These examples illustrate how assigning rough percentages for the probability of the truth of your beliefs allows you to hold them with integrity and humility throughout your life. This technique can also enable you to be more understanding and tolerant of those who hold beliefs different from your own.

- Consider one last example. Michael takes a different path from these three, a path followed by many believers. Michael has been a devout conservative Christian his whole life. In his early twenties, he began questioning parts of his beliefs that didn't seem to make sense, as did many of his friends. But the more he read and questioned, both philosophically and scientifically, the more he felt as if he were about to fall into an existential abyss.

  He feared that if he continued to go where the questions and answers were leading, he would no longer believe, and life would have no meaning. So he quickly backed off, and dove back into his very conservative version of Christianity. Now, if anyone questions what he believes to be the correct Christian doctrines, he becomes annoyed and answers them sarcastically. Some of his friends say that he has become even more rigid than before.

  Michael's wife is also a devout Christian, but unlike Michael, she has other priorities than theology. She can't understand why her husband gets angry with their friends who question, and has asked him to be kinder, telling Michael that they are sincere and can't help their tendency to doubt. But he can't seem to do this.

  What Michael hasn't yet realized is that there simply doesn't need to be an either/or choice between believing his particular doctrines and not believing at all. In fact, if Michael examined his doctrines carefully, he would realize that they express a first-century worldview of God, ethics, science, and humanity, and so it is not surprising that twenty centuries later, his belief in them sometimes gives way to doubts.

  In our view, a better path for Michael would be to trust God and pray for help and grace as he explores, rather than ignores, these issues.

Then, as an exercise, Michael might explore what it is like to begin assigning percentages of likelihood or unlikelihood to Christian doctrines he values, as well as to possibilities that he fears. At some point, having considered the possibility that God may be very different from the Lord he was taught to believe in, he might need to admit to himself that he thinks there's a 20 percent chance that the picture of God he's always had may not be accurate, or, God forbid, a 1 percent chance that God may not even exist. Of course, that also means that he can take comfort in the fact that he has a fairly high assurance, 99 percent in fact, that in some form, God is real.

If he continues his quest for truth, it is quite possible Michael will come to a better understanding of God that encompasses the realities of science and of ethics as he understands them, even if it leaves him less than 100 percent certain of the Christian doctrines he previously refused to question. He will then have to decide whether to be open with his church and family about his level of doubt. His church might not understand; his wife probably will. Either way, however, Michael will find he has more internal peace and a deeper faith as a result of acknowledging his doubts and questions.

Doubt as a Spiritual Practice

If you still wonder about the wisdom of examining your doubts rather than suppressing them, consider this.

Throughout history, especially in times of turmoil and economic uncertainty, large segments of the population have been inclined to turn to an absolutist version of their faith, to extreme nationalism, or to a toxic combination of the two, and hold on to it as a lifeline. They brook no dissent, and search their souls and those of their neighbors for any hint of disloyalty. In their zeal to punish those who they think are betraying the cause, they have committed crimes against neighbors, against nations, and against their God and themselves.

In the October 9, 2006, issue of *Time*, Andrew Sullivan argued that embracing spiritual doubt is a *necessity* for the peaceful coexistence of nations. In his essay, he wrote that the main reason Iran's then President, Mahmoud Ahmadinejad, was so dangerous wasn't because of his professed beliefs—his denial of the Holocaust and his eager anticipation of Armageddon—as appalling and alarming as those views were. It was because he genuinely seemed to have no doubts about them whatsoever. Even though he was, by then, unpopular in his own country and widely hated abroad, to all outward appearance he remained fanatically certain that his understanding of "the will of Almighty God" would prevail. Sullivan wrote:

> Many Western liberals and secular types look at the zealotry closing in on them and draw an obvious conclusion: religion is the problem. As our global politics become more enamored of religious certainty, the stakes have increased, they argue, and they have a point. The evil terrorists of al-Qaeda invoke God as the sanction for their mass murder. And many beleaguered Americans respond by invoking God's certainty. And the cycle intensifies into something close to a religious war. When the presidents of the U.S. and Iran speak as much about God as about diplomacy, we have entered a newly dangerous era. The [fundamentalist] Islamist resurgence portends the worst.

Imagine the fanaticism of sixteenth-century Christians, how they waged religious wars and burned heretics at the stake. Now give them nukes. See the problem?

Domestically, the resurgence of religious certainty has deepened our cultural divisions. And so our political discourse gets more polarized, and our global discourse gets close to impossible.

> How, after all, can you engage in a rational dialogue with a man like Ahmadinejad, who believes that Armageddon is near and that it is his duty to accelerate it? How can Israel negotiate with people who are certain their instructions come from heaven and so decree that Israel must not exist in Muslim lands? Equally, of course, how can one negotiate with fundamentalist Jews who claim that the West Bank is theirs forever by biblical mandate? Or with Fundamentalist Christians who believe that Israel's expansion is a biblical necessity rather than a strategic judgment?[28]

Such fanatical certainty isn't exclusive to the Abrahamic faiths. It can wreak havoc in even the most peaceful and open religions. Myanmar is a predominantly Buddhist nation; Buddhism is doctrinally a tolerant and peace-seeking faith. In spite of that, Myanmar's Buddhist majority has long practiced discrimination against its Muslim minority, a situation that has often flared into anti-Muslim riots, mosque-burnings, and massacres, usually egged on by fundamentalist Buddhist monks. (How, you may ask, can Buddhist "fundamentalists" justify acts that are the very opposite of their fundamental beliefs? They are claiming that because their faith is true, the absolutist beliefs and practices of Muslims must be suppressed, rather than looking for the values that unite them to Muslims and other traditions).

What can be done? Sullivan concludes that the answer to the problem of religious fanatics must be sought in the religions themselves:

> There is, however, a way out. And it will come from the only place it can come from—the minds and souls of people of faith. It will come from the much-derided moderate Muslims, tolerant Jews, and humble Christians. The alternative to the secular-fundamentalist death spiral is something called spiritual humility and sincere religious doubt. Fundamentalism is not the only valid form of faith, and to say it is, is the great lie of our time.[29]

After all, none of us is infallible. Therefore, doubt in the form of a deep humility about our beliefs should be a spiritual practice for *all of us*, regardless of our faith or nonfaith. Truly, the believing skeptics and the skeptical believers among us have an important role to play in the evolution of religion today.

9

Holy Books and Miracles

Assumptions that have traditionally surrounded our concepts of the scriptures and the sacred—assumptions that are no longer commonly believed in most of Europe—are still accepted in much of the United States. We need to rethink these assumptions. The reasons why should not surprise anyone who has walked the journey with us to this point.

In the past 200 years, American Christians have used various Bible passages to argue

- for the continuation of slavery
- for poll taxes in the past, and more currently gerrymandering and voter suppression laws to prevent Black people from voting
- against giving women the right to vote and own property
- against allowing Jews, Blacks, Mexicans, Chinese, and others to go to their schools or live in their neighborhoods
- against interracial marriages
- against civil rights for nonheterosexuals, and more.

Usually, when there's been a call for a newer understanding of society, morality, or creation, these traditionalists have fought it, citing the Bible to support their position. They sincerely believe that their faith makes them better people, and their communities better places to live—places where sin and evil are much less likely to gain a foothold.

Yet the data suggest a different reality. In general, the most religious states have higher rates of poverty, teen pregnancy, domestic violence, gun deaths, and other social ills than the least religious states.

Now that we have made major strides in learning how nature truly works, it is counterproductive to rely exclusively on ancient holy texts for science, history, and ethics, especially when they contradict reality.

In this chapter we focus on the Bible, the most influential sacred text for Western civilization. But the points we discuss could be raised for scriptures from other faiths as well. All ancient sacred texts illustrate the divine mysteries with analogies from the natural world, and so they all contain scientifically inaccurate descriptions and explanations, because the ancient writers didn't understand the natural world in the way that we do today.

Ancient scriptures also sometimes contain moral and social prescriptions that today we find reprehensible: harsh, rigid caste systems; savage punishments for small crimes; ostracism or even elimination of the physically and mentally afflicted. The times these laws were written in were harsher; the societies they were written for were menaced by diseases and disasters and violent human drives that ancient peoples were not able to understand as fully as we do now.

Yet the same ancient scriptures also offer much wisdom, beauty, joy, wonder, peace, and encouragement to act with love and justice toward others. That's because, in spite of the limitations in human experience that these books reflect, they also reflect the deep and insightful responses of their writers to a heightened experience of the sacred.

Sacred *and* Human in Origin

Part of the problem is the assumption that a book like the Bible is *either* sacred *or* human in origin. It is both. The sacred is speaking with and through the humans who wrote the words. The books that make up the Bible are a series of spiritual revelations recorded by human beings who were products of their times and places.

Most of the Bible's writers thought that the earth was flat, covered with a domed sky; that epilepsy, schizophrenia, and other such diseases were caused by demonic possession; that heaven was a literal place above the clouds; and so on. Taking *all* of their writings literally would be scientifically foolish. In many cases, it would also be unethical.

Before the United States even existed, those who claimed to follow the teachings of Christ used specific Bible passages to argue that the Inquisition was God's will; that the Crusades—which involved pillaging, killing, and raping civilians in addition to battling Muslim armies—were a holy war; that slavery was lawful; that women should not have basic human rights, and that adulterers and gay men should be put to death; that disabled people must have sinned to deserve their disabilities; that witches were real and should be burned alive; and that Jews who refused to worship Jesus should be tortured to death. And that is only a partial list.

Although each of these beliefs was based on literal words and examples from somewhere in the Bible, each one is also in direct opposition to the message and life of Jesus and the deepest truths spoken by the Old Testament prophets. So when adherents of certain Jewish and Christian traditions rejected slavery, the killing of nonbelievers, the inferior status of women, and so on, they returned to the scriptures to reconsider the texts on those topics in the light of the deeper biblical core values of compassion, justice, and peace.

Bibliolatry

That is the way any holy text *must* be approached. If, after careful consideration, you realize that a passage does not give a satisfactory account of what you know to be morally or scientifically true, then you should pause and reconsider it. To dogmatically affirm what is problematic is to make an idol out of the text, placing it above god and above ethics.

For example, women among the Bronze Age Semitic tribes had almost no civil rights. They were considered inferior to men and were treated like property. Polygamy was common. Not surprisingly, many Old Testament passages reflect this viewpoint. But that doesn't mean we should take that viewpoint as part of the holy revelation, any more than we accept the verses that imply that the earth is flat.

Here's another example: According to the Bible, God commanded Joshua to practice genocide—to kill every single Canaanite, including the children, so the Israelites could take over their lands. Was it because all Canaanites were evil, such that ridding the world of them would be a good thing, as some Bible commentators have suggested? We reject that view. (Modern archaeology has provided evidence that although Israelites had their own cultural identity, they were, in fact, ethnic Canaanites who had lived in Canaan since the middle of the twelfth century BCE, as the Ammonites, Moabites, and Phoenicians had been.)

Demonizing one's enemy in the name of one's God has always helped justify acts of war—it still goes on today. Religious skeptics may ask, "Why bother trying to sugarcoat ridiculous or toxic beliefs? What's the point of even reading these so-called sacred texts, other than for historical interest?" We suggest a twofold answer to these questions:

- Practically speaking, many believers are not willing to give up their holy books, so it behooves us, and especially those of us who are fellow believers but value current science and ethics, to provide this response as well.

- There are tremendous riches of wisdom, solace, and inspiration in these texts that many millions of people have found deeply moving and sustaining through the ages. Many of the core principles expressed in these books are key to helping us love each other and work to heal the world's ills. It is the holy books themselves, in fact, that teach us to reconsider and reject what is savage, petty, and outdated in them. Just as living creatures do, these books carry within them the process and energy—the DNA—of their own positive evolution.

Whose Authority?

Christian believers often object: "If the Bible isn't your ultimate authority, how will you be able to decide what's moral and what's not?" To that we respond, again, that the Bible was written in a sacred-human partnership. Therefore, it is a major mistake to see the Bible's authority as absolute. That not only leads to immoral laws, customs, and actions, but also to bibliolatry (the worship of the Bible above God), and idolatry is also a biblical prohibition.

Conservative Christians present their positions on morality and society as biblical and therefore immutable. Yet history shows that moral issues, such as those surrounding sexuality, marriage, and food taboos, have continually changed, and even changed within the centuries during which the Bible was written. Polygamy and the treatment of women as property were acceptable and normal when many of the Old Testament books were written, but by New Testament times, those norms had begun changing. Slavery was considered morally acceptable in both the Old and New Testaments, but verses such as Galatians 3:28 ("there is neither slave nor free . . . for you are all one in Christ") indicate that the institution was beginning to be questioned even before the New Testament was completed.

Even American Christian morality has changed dramatically in just a few generations. Back in the 1960s, drinking, dancing, and playing cards were frowned upon in many Christian circles, and divorce was uniformly condemned. Many churches even prohibited divorced people who had remarried from being members, and if you were a pastor who'd divorced, you had to look for a new career.

1980: A Dramatic Change for American Evangelicals

That changed with the Republican presidential nomination of 1980. Ronald Reagan drank, danced, and played cards, all in moderation, of course. He had not only been divorced and remarried, but he had also signed the nation's first no-fault divorce law as California's governor.

Having cast their lot with Reagan in the 1980 election, conservative Christians eased up on their routine prohibitions, and their uniform condemnations of divorce all but disappeared. Jerry Falwell and other conservative preachers of that era continued to attack abortion, feminism, and homosexuality, but for the most part, they stopped including divorce in their laundry list of sins. This is especially ironic considering that Jesus was quite clear about his views on divorce ("Anyone who divorces his wife, except for sexual immorality, and marries another woman commits adultery"[30]), but he never mentioned abortion, feminism, or homosexuality.

This is not to say divorce is either morally neutral or always wrong. Divorce can often be devastating, especially when children are involved. The point is that a blanket condemnation of divorce was never helpful, nor was forcing people to remain in harmful marriages—often as harmful to the children as to the parents. Fortunately, American Christian moral views changed to reflect that reality, even among the conservatives who claimed that their biblical morality was immutable.

Our biological heritage, we have seen, makes us susceptible to behaving in ways that are unjust, unloving, and stupid, so that we make mistakes that hurt ourselves and others, even those we love the most. As we discussed in Chapter 5 ("Neuroscience"), acknowledging the realities of this heritage makes us better able to take steps to effectively deal with our counterproductive and destructive tendencies.

Acknowledging our heritage also makes us more truthful and rational about the realities of our own lives. Widely used personality tests such as the Minnesota Multiphasic Personality Inventory (MMPI) indicate that extremely religious people tend to give more false answers than do less religious or nonreligious people.[31]

Mental health researchers believe that the reason is that those with strong belief systems answer the questions based on how they wish and believe things were, instead of how they actually are. This is why so many conservative believers accuse progressives of practicing moral relativism, in contrast to their own biblically based morality, which they say "is the same yesterday, today, and forever"—in spite of the overwhelming evidence that what people call biblically based morality has changed and continues to change significantly over time.

If you really want to see a quantum leap in concepts of morality, look at the "Sacred Morality?" sidebar on the facing page. It lists a small sampling of the many biblical passages that attribute commands to God that are clearly immoral by today's standards, but were perfectly moral in the eyes of the ancient scribes who wrote our scriptures. Each culture in each era wrestles with its own ethical issues, based on its own current scientific knowledge and level of social awareness. To believe that the morality of an ancient sacred text is absolute for all time is naïve; it denies the progress in understanding that humanity has made over time.

Jesus himself was a creative genius at grappling with and redefining traditional Jewish beliefs and the "You have heard it said" culture and morality of his time. Many of his teachings began, "You have heard it said . . . But I say . . ." Instead of obeying the letter of the law, Jesus called his listeners to look at the state of their hearts. And he embraced those outside the tribe, including those considered unclean by the Torah's rigid purity codes—lepers, menstruating women, and others who were at that time considered untouchable.

Sacred Morality?

According to the Bible, the rules and "facts" below were decreed by God. Old Testament leaders such as Joshua enforced these rules as they slaughtered their enemies. They believed that obeying these rules and affirming these "facts" brought favor from God, and that God would bless them with victories in their battles.

1. If a city or group opposes us and doesn't do what we believe God requires, or refuses to convert to our religion, we will kill all of them—men, women, and children—unless we have a need for slaves or wives, in which case, we'll take the women for our slaves, concubines, and wives.[32]
2. Whether we are at war or not, we will slaughter anyone who doesn't worship God in the way that we believe is true—it is God's command.[33]
3. Women must be under the authority of a man, whether their father, brother, or husband, and they are not entitled to the rights that men have under the law. (This is in both the Old and New Testaments. The New Testament adds that women can, however, go to heaven if they have children.[34])
4. Likewise, children have no rights, especially daughters. In fact, if a family falls on hard times and needs to raise money, the father may sell a daughter to someone desiring a slave or a wife.[35]
5. Sons who defy their parents should be put to death.[36]
6. Misfortunes and illnesses, including mental illnesses, are caused by demons[37] and sin.[38]
7. Some of the many "abominations" that cause misfortune, illness, and death are eating shrimp, lobster,[39] or pork,[40] and performing male homosexual acts—in fact, any man who commits a homosexual act should be put to death.[41]

Israelite warlords such as Joshua have truthfully claimed to be following the Bible when imposing such rules on those whom they have conquered. Notes 32 through 41 for this chapter cite the actual Bible verses that justify the beliefs and actions we list. They are only a fraction of the verses in the Bible that are ethically reprehensible by civilized, modern standards.

In short, if you are using the *entire* Bible as the authority for your morality, you are committed to values that most humans today would condemn as grossly immoral.

Part Two: Religion Comes of Age

The Bible's Changing Definition of God

Not only do our definitions of morality and our worldviews change over time, so do our definitions of God. Even within the Old Testament one finds at least four evolving concepts of God. They are a fascinating record of humanity's spiritual development from our earliest eras.

Initially, the God of the Israelites was simply their local tribal deity. Being a loyal Israelite meant worshiping that god, instead of some other local tribe's god. Later, Israelite religious leaders claimed that their God was more powerful than the other gods, and that when they went to war, their God would help them win. If they didn't win, it wasn't because their enemies were more powerful or had better weapons. It was because the people of Israel had been unfaithful to their God.

Still later, Israelites began to conceive of their God as the supremely powerful creator of everything, and felt that no other tribe or nation should be allowed to put their gods above God. From there it was a short step to monotheism: the God of Israel was the *only* God; other gods didn't even exist. All four understandings of God—tribal deity, superior god, supreme God, and only God—are intermingled in different Old Testament passages. Furthermore, the images of God range from a jealous, angry, capricious, warlike tyrant to a loving, peacemaking, generous creator and sustainer.

Then, of course, came Christ, and those of his disciples who believed in the divinity of their teacher and the divine authority of his teachings. They eventually expanded the definition of God to encompass Jesus. By the fourth century, some three hundred years after Christ, Christians had come to see their One God as a Sacred Trinity: Father, Son, and Holy Spirit. Well before then, they had also begun to supplement the divine with a pantheon of saints, each equipped to succor some special human distress or fill some human need, somewhat like the Olympian gods of polytheistic Greece and Rome.

Today, new pictures of god are emerging, pictures that better fit with a twenty-first-century understanding of the world. In the previous chapters, we described god as both indwelling and encompassing everything in the cosmos. That picture works well within most of the faith traditions, except in the most fundamentalist branches.

We also made the case that if you look at the broad sweep of how creation and evolution have proceeded, it becomes increasingly difficult to believe that such a god would interact with creation in supernatural ways that contradict natural laws. So that brings us to the Bible's miraculous and supernatural claims. What about those? And in the case of Jesus, what about the claim that he not only performed miracles, like Moses and other Old Testament prophets, but that he performed them on his own initiative, using his own powers, because he is actually God?

Jesus or Christ?

There is a common misperception that holy figures such as Jesus, the Buddha, and Mohammad created the religions associated with them. They did not create their religions; their followers did. Jesus is unique among them because his followers eventually claimed that he was "fully God" as well as a prophet.

A passage in *Mere Christianity*, by C.S. Lewis, is often quoted by those who argue for the divinity of Jesus: "A man who was merely a man and said the sort of things Jesus said would not be a great moral teacher," wrote Lewis.

> He would either be a lunatic—on the level with a man who says he is a poached egg—or he would be the devil of hell. You must take your choice. Either this was, and is, the Son of God, or else a madman or something worse. You can shut him up for a fool or you can fall at his feet and call him Lord and God. But let us not come with any patronizing nonsense about his being a great human teacher. He has not left that open to us.[42]

In truth, however, the historical Jesus never claimed to be God. In the 1940s and 1950s, when Lewis was writing these words, biblical scholars were only just beginning to reach a consensus that a number of claims attributed to Jesus in the New Testament were not actually words that Jesus said. Lewis might not have been familiar with that scholarship, but ironically, most pastors today are well aware of it, because they have studied the New Testament in seminary. Many of them do not share this scholarship with their congregations, however, for fear they will be labeled heretics.

The historical Jesus was a reform-minded itinerant Jewish preacher who proclaimed a message of relational love, offered healing to the suffering and liberation to the oppressed, and most of all inspired in his followers a tremendous love and desire to follow his teachings. He also believed—wrongly, as it turns out—that the end-times would come in his lifetime. He lit the spark that the apostle Paul most famously fanned into flame: the fire that became the Christianity that declared us all *one*, whether we were kosher or not, male or female, rich or poor, slaves or free. It became the faith that eventually elevated Jesus to the position of "the Christ."

Putting Words in the Mouth of Jesus

"Jesus, the Second Person of the Godhead" refers to the belief that Jesus is the divine Messiah, the Christ, the Son of God, who was literally brought back to physical life on the third day after his death on the cross, who was with God from the beginning, and through whom all things were made.

The Gospel of John, which was written after the other three Gospels, describes this Jesus most clearly, and in it Jesus makes the statements that conform to this picture. Scholars have established clearly that, as was common and acceptable in that era, the writer of the Gospel of John put words in Christ's mouth to make his points. One reason we know this is that the speech patterns and word choices of John's Jesus are completely different from Jesus's way of speaking in all the earliest records of his words, including the earlier Gospels—Matthew, Mark, and Luke.

These three Gospels, although they also sometimes allude to a divine understanding of Jesus, do so to a much less developed extent than John's Gospel. And they do not claim that Jesus called himself divine.

In fact, the earliest known version of Mark, the first Gospel written, appears to explain the resurrection of Jesus as the heavenly resurrection of his soul, rather than his literal revival on earth, body and all. It also ends much more abruptly than the version of Mark that we have today. Certain Christians were so dissatisfied with Mark's conclusion in chapter 16 that they added verses 9 through 20 around the early second century.

What About Sightings of the Risen Jesus?

However, several other New Testament books do recount sightings of Jesus after his death. Where did those stories come from?

There is one obvious way that the earliest disciples differed from subsequent believers: they knew Jesus as a fellow human extremely well, having lived and traveled with him for at least three years. Imagine being on the road and facing trials, irritations, dirt, crowds, and the need to obtain food and clothes when you have no steady means of support, month after month, year after year. The fact that the disciples' love, admiration, and devotion to Jesus not only remained steadfast under these circumstances, but also increased, makes it clear that he was truly someone special.

It is a commonly reported psychological phenomenon that when someone dies, their close friends and relatives will often have a sense that they are still present, regularly reporting visual and auditory experiences of their deceased loved one. Over time, the intensity of these experiences fades.

Why would losing Jesus be any different for the disciples? Might this explain why, according to the New Testament stories, Jesus appeared to some of his followers for a finite period, and then ceased his appearances? Maybe we need to take a less physical and more spiritual approach to the question of resurrection.

How Jesus Understood Himself

Based on extensive New Testament research, scholars conclude that *Christus* ("the Christ") was not actually how Jesus referred to himself. Of all the titles ascribed to Jesus in the New Testament, scholars think that "Son of Man" is the one Jesus most often used of himself. (The phrase appears 81 times in the Gospels, including 14 times in Mark.) The historical Jesus understood himself as a teacher and healer who proclaimed a Judaism with roots in the teachings of Rabbi Hillel the Elder's radical message of relational love: "That which is hateful to you, do not do to another; that is the entire Torah, and the rest is its interpretation."[43]

In short, Jesus did not create Christianity with himself as God; his followers did. After all, some of the powerful leaders of the first century, including the Roman emperor, were considered divine beings, and sometimes were even considered to have been born of a virgin. Why should the disciples' beloved leader be any different? Yet it took quite a while before the divinity of Jesus became a widely accepted article of faith.

That's because there was much more diversity and ferment in early Christianity than most of us realize. In an introduction to a chapter on the Gospel of Mary Magdalene, in one of the first translations of this ancient text for the English-speaking public, Cynthia Bourgeault writes that acknowledgment of the diversity at the heart of early Christianity is "a fairly recent breakthrough in Biblical scholarship." She continues:

> Even a generation ago, leading scholars ... approached these texts under the sway of a mindset so entrenched that it can rightfully be called the Christian 'master story.' We are now able to see more

clearly that 'the master story' is simply the view from the winner's circle, and that texts which had earlier been perceived as deviants from a presumed original orthodoxy are in fact authentic testaments to the pluralism at the heart of early Christianity, culturally as well as theologically. And its pluralism is not a cause for dismay; rather it is a huge new boost of hope as Christianity struggles today to emerge from a two-thousand-year-old Greco-Roman cosmovision that has become... far too narrow to convey the energy, much less the truth, of the original vision of Jesus.[44]

When Jesus Became God: The Master Story According to Constantine

The early 300s were the crucial turning point at which this "master story" took hold. In 313 CE, the Roman Emperor Constantine (whose mother was a Christian) proclaimed the decriminalization of Christianity in what was the first step toward its eventual position as the official religion of the Roman Empire.

By 325 CE, after years of often murderous political infighting among various Christian factions over a series of hotly contested dogmas, such as whether Jesus was God or human or a combination of the two, Constantine convened the Council of Nicaea. He commanded the approximately 300 church leaders in attendance to come up with an official version of Christianity in order to stop the inter-Christian slaughter and disruption of the peace.

The result? Jesus as the Christ was finally codified in what we now know as the Nicene Creed: "God from God, Light from Light, true God from true God, begotten, not made, of one being with the Father." By Constantine's order, all church leaders who disagreed with this creed were to be exiled and excommunicated, and their writings were to be burned. Anyone found possessing these heretical writings was to be executed. Not surprisingly, dissent and fighting among the various Christian factions calmed down (although it has never disappeared), and belief in Jesus as one with God and other elements of the master story were on their way to becoming widely accepted.

It is beyond the scope of this book to delve into the fascinating account of how our current creeds came into being and how the texts that now make up the New Testament were chosen from the approximately 5,500 often conflicting manuscripts about Jesus that were in circulation at

Holy Books and Miracles

that time. We recommend the books of leading New Testament authorities such as Bart D. Ehrman, John Dominic Crossan, and the late Marcus Borg for those interested in learning more about this subject.

Jesus, the Spiritual Leader

As we have seen, the historical Jesus was a reform-minded rabbi who proclaimed a message of love, healing, and liberation. Whether or not you believe he was divine, it is clear he was one of the world's greatest and most influential spiritual leaders. But for a rapidly growing number of us, his resurrection was not the literal resurrection of a man whose corpse was revived, walked the earth for 40 days, and then rose into the sky and disappeared behind a cloud (Acts 1:9). Rather, we celebrate the resurrection of the spirit of an incredible teacher who still inspires his followers to spread love, justice, and healing throughout the world.

That does not mean we see Jesus's resurrection as a purely human affair. In fact, we think the spirit of his resurrection has everything to do with the many things we call "sacred." The authors of this book hold different views on what it means for the spirit of Jesus to continue to exist, as do many others who have researched and thought about this question over the centuries. Profound mysteries are like that. We learn to rest with the ambiguities of our faith, far beyond certainty.

What About the Miracles of Jesus?

In Appendix B, on miracles, connected with Chapter 6 ("An Omnipresent God"), we write about people known as healers. When healers suggest more constructive, life-giving ways of thinking, or place their hands on a person who is seeking emotional or physical healing, the person feels the warmth and a sense of well-being from the healer's attention and often gets better, sometimes dramatically better. The human mind has an extraordinary capacity for self-healing in ways that are fully consistent with the natural order. The more gifted the healer is in understanding others and influencing their sense of release and peace, the more powerful and frequent are the resulting healings.

We contend that Jesus must have been this kind of healer, because so many people desired his touch. We see no reason to deny the spirituality and sacredness of these healings, and for some of us, it is very natural to use the word god or God when we speak of healing. But it is also clear that Jesus recognized the need for the people he touched to have faith in the process in order for it to be effective. In many of the Gospel accounts, he is quoted as saying, "your faith has made you well." Jesus must have understood the mutual participation of his spirit and that of the person he was healing. He must have been one of those people with a remarkable presence and power, a charisma so great that it transformed those around him. Proof may be impossible, but it is certainly plausible to believe that Jesus was one of those very few people—in India they are called *mahatmas*, or "great souls"—who deepen the sense of the presence of God for those around them. In fact, we think it is likely that Jesus was gifted in this way to a unique degree.

As for miracles such as Jesus feeding the five thousand, or walking on water during a storm, there is absolutely no way to prove whether these are true or not, or what might have been true that gained or changed in the telling and retelling. Those of us who believe that Jesus did not break the laws of nature view these stories as some of the many legends that sprang up among early Christians who had been profoundly touched by Jesus, and who interpreted his power and charisma as signs of his divinity.

These stories could well have had a basis in something that actually happened. For example, many have suggested that the feeding of the five thousand took place when people were inspired to share the food they had with others after they saw the boy offer his loaves and fishes to Jesus. In fact, activist Sister Simone Campbell (of Nuns on the Bus fame) likes to joke that the reason the Gospel of Matthew says, "five thousand men were fed to say nothing of women and children," was because Matthew was only counting the ones who thought it was a miracle. All the women had brought food from home to share, so they knew where it came from. But the men said, "Wow, food; what a miracle!"

Disciples who were fishing may have been fearful when a sudden storm came up, and felt comforted when they saw Jesus walking along the shore. With the waves whipping up the water between them, it could well have appeared that Jesus was walking on water. Again, we can't know for sure, but if we want to interpret the God-world relationship in a way that's consistent with science, we'll have to seek an understanding of Jesus's miracles that is consistent with natural laws.

Can You Be a Christian Without Believing in the Supernatural?

All Christians attempt to follow the teachings of Jesus as they understand them, regardless of whether or not they believe in his divinity. Although many of the world's Christians still hold that the only acceptable understanding of Jesus is "the Second Person of the Godhead," a significant and growing number are drawn to see Jesus in a wider variety of ways.

For some, Jesus is a gifted spiritual and ethical teacher or rabbi, but not more. For some, he is a role model; for some, a prophetic advocate of justice; for some, a human being deeply attuned to the divine Spirit. Some experience him as being the presence of God in a unique way, such that the Spirit of Christ continues to be present wherever God is present. In addition to the other roles, he is also the Immanuel, "God with us," of Jewish and Christian tradition.

Most of us, despite our differences, seek to follow "Jesus, the spiritual teacher and model" because we value his teachings and see him as a central part of our spiritual heritage. More than previous generations, we are pluralists, undisturbed by the conclusions that different people reach about who Jesus was, whether he was extraordinary, and, if yes, what made him exceptional. We are not disturbed that other Christians think about Jesus differently than we do. And we do not find it necessary to judge or condemn members of other religious traditions for following other teachers, or for finding their spiritual home in other beliefs and practices.

To use a phrase from Jesus's Sermon on the Mount, it seems better to concentrate on the beam (plank) in our own eye than on the mote (speck of sawdust) in the eye of another. Interestingly, advanced practitioners in a particular spiritual tradition are often the *least* inclined to condemn serious practitioners from other traditions.

Many European Christians are more drawn to the spiritual and ethical interpretations of Jesus than they are to the supernatural ones. In recent decades, the number of American Christians also adopting this approach has increased dramatically. When the Episcopal bishop John Shelby Spong began defending this understanding of Jesus in the 1980s, his writings were viewed as controversial, even scandalous. By 2013, the Very Reverend Gary Hall, dean of the National Cathedral in Washington, DC, could publicly acknowledge that he held similar views, something that would have been unheard-of even a few decades ago.

PART TWO: RELIGION COMES OF AGE

Unnecessary Divisions

Even today, there are many on the Jesus-is-God side of the Christian spectrum who repudiate those of us on the Jesus-the-Spiritual-Leader side as non-Christians, describing us as heretics, possibly even hell-bound heretics. This is unfortunate.

To our conservative colleagues we make this plea: If you want to hold fast to your beliefs about Jesus as God, fine, but please don't deride us for reaching the conclusions that we are compelled to reach. We must investigate the questions that surface as we confront tensions between traditional ancient beliefs and the realities of science and the natural world, and we must voice our concerns about the ethics of a traditional view of God. You can define your own discipleship without condemning our understanding of what it means to live according to the way of Jesus.

Jesus offers an amazing message and path for the complex world of the twenty-first century. And no theologian or creed will ever give us the final formulation of what his message means. We need to draw on every resource that we can find. If we spend our time drawing lines in the sand, proclaiming "in" and "out," we silence voices that could help us interpret that ancient message for today.

Conservatives may love neat, exclusive categories, but clearly Jesus did not. Nor is our world neat and tidy. Young people in particular are increasingly skeptical of ultimatum dichotomies of this sort. As conservative Christian leaders cling more and more tightly to views that contradict science and current ethical thinking, they become the instruments of their own demise.

Many good, thinking people come to reject rigid interpretations of faith and to leave the churches that preach them, a decision that could well be a step *toward* spiritual health. They can no longer accept doctrines that Jesus likely wouldn't have accepted either, had he been born today.

People who leave their church for such reasons are usually not giving up faith altogether. Rather, they are seeking a more believable faith, one that stands up to scrutiny in the light of modern knowledge and an evolved ethical and social understanding. They are looking for communities that stand outside of traditional orthodoxy. People who would like to remain in the Christian tradition are looking to find Jesus in the way we relate with one another. They seek the Jesus who unites, without the dogmas that divide.

Instead of focusing on the contentious debates—*In what sense was Jesus God and in what sense a man? Was he resurrected physically or spiritually?*—wouldn't it be more fruitful to focus on living a life that embraces the words, actions, and spirit of Jesus?

Even twenty-first-century people who can no longer buy into the first-century picture of the world can still affirm that central message: to love our neighbor, to resist injustice and bigotry, and to tend to the concerns of the poor and marginalized. These are the ideals that draw even non-Christians toward leaders like Pope Francis or Sister Simone Campbell, who embody many values that people of goodwill from any belief system can embrace, whether or not they believe Jesus is divine.

10

The Afterlife

FOR MANY RELIGIONS, IT is an article of faith that our soul, spirit, or consciousness continues in some form after we die. A big reason for this belief is the amazing uniformity of near-death experiences (NDEs), reported by people from diverse religions, cultures, and historical eras.

We now have thousands of recorded accounts of NDEs. People, including children, stopped breathing, were considered technically dead, and then were revived. Only about 15 percent of people have such experiences, but those who do consider them deeply spiritual. They often believe they were about to enter heaven (or whatever their concept of afterlife was) before they returned to life, which they often did reluctantly. Nonreligious people also describe such experiences.

The most common NDEs involve being drawn or led through a tunnel toward a bright light; briefly reuniting with dead loved ones, including pets or a figure in one's religion; and, about one-fourth of the time, watching medical staff trying to resuscitate you. Other NDEs are much rarer.

Testing NDEs

To open the section of this chapter about NDEs, we picked Dr. Sam Parnia, a respected medical doctor who is described as "one of the world's leading experts on the scientific study of death and near-death experiences."[45]

He wrote a widely read book on NDEs and collaborated with a number of other healthcare providers on the following experiment.

The medical staff placed images on a shelf facing the ceilings of rooms where cardiac-arrest patients typically underwent resuscitation efforts. Their goal: if the survivors who described having an out-of-body experience could describe the images, they'd know their out-of-body experience wasn't just a hallucination triggered in their brain from a TV show or movie that depicted a medical team using a defibrillator to start someone's heart.

Nothing ever came of this experiment. After 2,060 cardiac arrests with 330 survivors, only nine remembered NDEs, and one reported an out-of-body experience. But the man who had the out-of-body experience was in a room with no images.

Elisabeth Kübler-Ross's Defense of NDEs

So, we returned to the gold standard, the late Dr. Elisabeth Kübler-Ross, whose compassion, intelligence, and observatory skills were second to none. Fortunately, she wrote down most of her observations. She began her psychiatric residency at Manhattan State Hospital and completed it in 1963 at the University of Colorado School of Medicine and then moved to Chicago. Like other medical experts who were monitoring NDEs in the late 1970s and early 1980s, Kübler-Ross theorized that the pain-killing endorphins that flooded her patients' bodies while they went through trauma, along with the oxygen deprivation from lack of blood to the brain, created the euphoria and consciousness-expanding experiences the survivors were describing. Certain kinds of seizures and various hallucinogenic drugs can provide similar experiences.

Michael Shermer, founding publisher of *Skeptic* magazine and author of several *New York Times* best sellers that debunk widely held beliefs, is skeptical of stronger claims that Kübler-Ross later made in defense of NDEs. In his *Why People Believe Weird Things*, he writes, "It seems obvious that these [NDEs] were hallucinatory wishful-thinking experiences, yet Kübbler-Ross went out of her way to verify these stories. She did not buy the prosaic explanation. What she noticed immediately was that patients who were having out-of-body experiences were watching from a position outside and above."[46]

Shermer cites another argument from Kübler-Ross:

"You have totally blind people," said Kübler-Ross, "who don't even have light perception, don't even see shades of gray. If they have an NDE, they can report exactly what the scene looked like at the accident or hospital room. How do you explain that?"

Shermer answers Kübler-Ross's question: "Simple: Memories of verbal descriptions given by others during the NDE were converted into visual images of the scene and rendered back into words. Further, quite frequently patients in trauma or surgery are not totally unconscious . . . they are aware of what is happening around them. If the patient is in a teaching hospital, [the teaching staff] would be describing the procedure for the other residents, thus enabling the patient to give an accurate description of events."[47]

Simply Synapses?

Kübler-Ross ultimately believed that NDEs are real and suggested ways that their authenticity might be demonstrated. In response, Shermer and others have worked to show that it is possible that the various experiences she describes could have come from inside the patients' heads. Although believers and skeptics continue to hotly debate the veracity of NDEs, we should probably conclude that NDEs neither prove nor disprove the existence of an afterlife, although hope of an afterlife certainly offers comfort in the face of death. If there is a story to tell about continued existence after death in union with the divine, we, the authors, think it will be told in spiritual terms. There may well be a "thinning of the veil" in NDEs. But it won't be science that establishes what's on the other side of the veil.

Whether you tend to place greater emphasis on the scientific or the spiritual data about death and dying, the most constructive way to live is not to focus on our eventual escape from this world, but rather to fully engage with the world. That's also the takeaway for the people who have had NDEs. We are more fulfilled when we're working to co-create our present and future, to maximize love, joy, peace, justice, and a better world for our children and every other creature on this planet. All of these goals are valuable, whatever we believe about what comes afterward.

The Afterlife

And Then There's Hell

Many people believe hell is just a relic of primitive times when coercive religious leaders used the fear of it to control people. The threat of hellfire made the followers of these clerics more likely to obey civil and religious laws in this life to avoid punishment in the next.

There are certainly plenty of examples, both ancient and contemporary, of religious leaders using the threat of hell to motivate changes in behavior. When leaders today claim that only certain people are saved from damnation, those destined to be saved often seem to be the ones who most obediently follow these leaders' particular teachings.

Today, about 61 percent of Americans still believe in hell as a literal place, even if most don't believe they are going there. So it seems worth examining.

A very common version of conservative Christianity says that God our Father is so perfect that he can't even look at us in our sinful state. So, He sacrificed Jesus, his own Son, to die a terrible death in our stead. Once you accept Jesus as your personal savior, God will welcome you into his family and you will be saved from eternal torment. Otherwise, you can't be reconciled with God, and you are consequently hell-bound.

To put it mildly, this picture of God is not exactly the picture of a loving Father under our usual definition of love. It is also hard to understand how a deeply compassionate and essentially good God could go forward with his creation, knowing that billions and billions of future people were destined for a state of eternal torment.

Instead of hell, the Old Testament and the Torah used "Sheol," the ancient name for the place you went when you died, whether you were righteous or not. The afterlife wasn't a focus for most of the Old Testament writers; they were chiefly concerned with life here on earth.

The New Testament is scattered with about a half dozen references to "Hades," the Greek equivalent of "Sheol," as well. However, it also uses the much stronger word "Gehenna" about a dozen times, and "Gehenna" is rightly translated as "hell." It references Jerusalem's city dump, which had a constantly burning fire to incinerate trash, cadavers, and filth, and wild animals fought over scraps along its edges. It was truly a frightful place of "eternal fire" and "gnashing of teeth."[48]

Jesus and Hell

Oddly enough, almost every mention of this worse kind of hell is made by Jesus. Why? After all, Jesus is the one who emphasized God as a loving parent, denounced the "eye for an eye and tooth for a tooth" system of justice, and proclaimed, "Judge not." Is our Jesus the Spiritual Leader model in trouble? Was he using the concept of hell to manipulate people and bend them to his will, as too many ancient religious leaders and demagogues have done?

When you look at the context, the answer is an emphatic no. In fact, there are at least two ways to look at this kind of hell that fit with our scientific knowledge and with the concept of a good god.

Hell on Earth

Rob Bell, best-selling author, does an excellent job of addressing the concept of hell on earth in his book *Love Wins*.

> When people say they don't believe in hell and they don't like the word *sin*, my first response is to ask, "Have you sat and talked with a family who just found out their child has been molested? Repeatedly? Over a number of years? By a relative?"
>
> Some words are strong for a reason. We need those words to be that intense, loaded, complex, and offensive, because they need to reflect the realities they describe.
>
> And that's what we find with Jesus's words . . . He uses hyperbole often—telling people to gouge out their eyes and maim themselves rather than commit certain sins. It can all sound a bit over-the-top at times, even violent.
>
> But when you see the concentric rings of pain that are going to emanate from [someone's terrible choices], Jesus's warnings don't seem that over-the-top, they seem spot-on. Some agony needs agonizing language.[49]

That's what Jesus is doing with Luke's story of the rich man and Lazarus, according to Bell.[50] He is using hyperbole to show how warped the rich man's point of view is. Ludicrously, even in hell the rich man still expects Lazarus to come down from heaven and serve him. Abraham, who is cradling Lazarus in this parable, forbids it, telling the rich man that there is a chasm between the two places across which no one can pass.

Bell also examines each of the other occasions when Jesus brings up hell. In every case, he says, the main theme is that we are all brothers and sisters, children of the God who shows no favoritism. When we reject people like Lazarus, we are rejecting God.

Jesus, says Bell, is using "brilliant, surreal, poignant, subversive, loaded stories" to make his point. Hell is the metaphor Jesus uses for the torment we live in when we are living only for ourselves and failing to love our neighbors.

"Jesus," says Bell, "did not use hell to try and compel 'heathens' and 'pagans' to believe in God so they wouldn't burn when they died. He talked about hell to very religious people to warn them about the consequences of straying from their God-given calling . . . to show the world God's love."

Although Bell makes the case that "love wins," however, he doesn't want to get rid of the word *hell*:

> We need a loaded, volatile, adequately violent, dramatic, serious word to describe the very real consequences we [and society] experience when we reject the good and true and beautiful life that God has for us. We need a word that refers to the big, wide, terrible evil that comes from the secrets hidden deep within our hearts all the way to the massive, society-wide collapse and chaos that comes when we fail to live in God's world God's way. And for that, the word 'hell' works quite well. Let's keep it.[51]

Does Our Consciousness Have an Afterlife?

Chapter 3 described how someday, about 7 billion years from now, our Sun will enter its last throes of life, bloating up into a red giant, consuming Mercury and Venus, and frying Earth in the process. If our descendants haven't colonized other parts of space by then, or moved Earth substantially farther away from the Sun, humanity will be lost. Every human then living, the remains of every human who ever died, will be burned up, their particles/waves scattered throughout the cosmos. But if our consciousness is not made up of particles/waves, if our consciousness is an enduring unity, in principle it could continue to exist even then, experiencing an afterlife in some sense.

The belief that a conscious god is indeed the ultimate reality, and that our individual consciousness continues in some way after death, has the advantage of working well with pluralism. It says that your religion and your belief (or lack of belief) matter most in terms of how much they enhance your interconnectedness with others.

Such an afterlife, in which goodness and justice win in the end, could also be wishful thinking, of course. That's what atheist and best-selling author Sam Harris believes. He points out that 9 million children die every year before they reach the age of five, and responds,

> This concept of the afterlife functions . . . as a substitute for really absorbing our predicament, which is that everyone is going to die; there are circumstances that are just catastrophically unfair; evil sometimes wins and injustice sometimes wins, and the only justice we are going to find in the world is the justice we make. We have an ethical responsibility to absorb this, really down to the soles of our feet.[52]

Both Death and Life Are Sacred

To insist that your eternal fate depends on having the right beliefs about something that is impossible for human beings to know is clearly counterproductive. It seems safe and reasonable to rule out the existence of an eternal pit full of fire and brimstone and dancing demons where people are tortured forever because of what they believed or did in the short span of time that they were humans. It also seems safe to trust that whatever happens after we die will not be terrible, whether our consciousness ends at the grave, or continues in some way after our death.

Whether there's an afterlife or not, we will live on through our families and those whom we've touched in our lives. And our bodies that lie decaying in the ground enable new growth to flourish. It is all part of the cycle of life.

It took a multibillion-year cycle of cosmic birth, death, and procreation through multiple generations of stars to sow the chemical abundance that made life here on Earth possible. Yet a lifesaving *Penicillium* mold can grow on a decaying piece of fruit in less than a day. Death continues to seed new life at every level of the cosmos, from the largest star to the smallest organism. So, in a sense, death, like life, is also sacred.

Focusing on a hereafter that is unknowable can lead to a neglect of the things that matter right now. Might not our brief existence here on earth be more meaningful if we engage fully with life, attempting to act in ways that enhance the common good in our own time and for future generations?

11

Science, Religion, and Sacred Stories

MOST OF US WOULD like to see ourselves as a part of a grand and meaningful story, one that encompasses everything from the birth of our universe 13.8 billion years ago up through the latest news and discoveries of our era. We yearn for a saga that embraces the grandeur of our cosmos and the challenges and joys of our existence—a story that makes sense of our stumbling attempts to live up to the deepest ideals, truths, and feelings of compassion that characterize humans at our best.

The story of the universe that we summarized in the previous chapters beautifully fulfills this yearning. Whether you call it Big History, the Epic of Evolution, or the Great Story, it is *our* creation story—the true story of our cosmic genesis—from the Big Bang's initial explosion of energy and particles through the emergence of the galaxies and the budding of Earth's first primitive life to the gradual flowering of complexity and consciousness that enables us to comprehend it all. It is an interconnected, cataclysmic, bursting forth of diversity, complexity, and creativity.

Understanding the Great Story enables us to celebrate the creativity that resides in each of us; to work to conserve the lovely, fragile planet entrusted to us; to study and explore the mysteries of the cosmos; to better understand why we are the way we are and how we can improve; and to co-create an enlightened future for our children, our children's children, and our fellow species. It is a sacred creation story that gives us meaning and purpose, a worthy vessel for our deepest yearnings.

Part Two: Religion Comes of Age

Today we understand the evolutionary emergence that has brought us to this place, yet many of humanity's ancient sacred stories still retain a strong hold on us. This is not surprising: These stories have been a repository of wisdom through the ages, and in some respects also of truth, and they remain an important part of our Great Story as well.

And Yet . . .

For centuries, effective leaders have been reinterpreting the age-old stories as cultures developed, values changed, and new knowledge emerged. Such reinterpretations are a vital necessity. Too often, individuals and societies continue to apply the long-venerated tales in ways that made sense thousands of years ago but that no longer guide or contribute to human happiness and moral progress. Unless we reconsider the meaning of these stories in the light of new knowledge and understanding, they will continue to reinforce beliefs and motivate actions that we now recognize as harmful. When we bring the stories out into the light and transform them, however, they can become a catalyst for positive change and an inspiring part of our continuing Great Story.

In the previous chapter, we saw how Rob Bell reinterpreted the concept of hell. For him as well as for many of the rest of us, the old hell with its sadistic devils and eternal torment not only defied belief but also negated the concept of a good God. His reinterpretation is morally relevant and psychologically credible because it focuses on an aspect of the story of hell that still has meaning today: the agony caused by evil.

This Brings Us to an Even Worse Problem: The Subjugation of Women *in the Name of God*

One of religion's most tragic failures, in terms of sheer numbers affected, is its perpetuation of the subjugation of women, overtly, in the name of God. This is a major and troubling issue of basic human rights, but it is much more than that. Given how interdependent we are, we will not be able to move ahead if we continue to leave behind half of the world's population.

International studies overwhelmingly show that greater gender equality makes for more peaceful, prosperous, and environmentally sustainable societies.[53] And the most violent, poverty-stricken, and backward societies are the most fundamentalist, a condition directly correlated with the least gender equality. Yet despite the demonstrable wholeness that gender equity brings, the bias against women persists.

That's because none of these facts are enough to convince religious fundamentalists to change their practices if their religious beliefs are not addressed. Their beliefs are the major factor driving the worst practices against women. And women are not the only ones who suffer from religion's patriarchal bias: People of different sexualities and fluid gender rarely appear in scriptural narratives, and when they do, they are most often cast in a negative light. (Philip and the Ethiopian eunuch in Acts 8:26–40 are a happy exception.)

One proven method for improving gender equity is by supporting and publicizing the female scholars who are challenging and reinterpreting the sacred texts and traditional beliefs that seem to define women as lesser beings. Such scholarship is well established in Christianity and Judaism, and it has produced measurable advances in the emancipation of Western women.

Hindu, Buddhist, Muslim, and other female academic scholars, as well as thousands of lay women, have also been working on these issues in their countries of origin. For years now, they have been producing significant scholarship and lay pamphlets that undercut fundamentalist appeals to religion as a justification for the subjugation of women, but for them it is more of an uphill battle than for their Western sisters. Or it used to be.

Texas, Too

Now that Texas has criminalized abortion, infant deaths caused by severe genetic and birth defects have risen in the state by 21.6 percent. In other words, in Texas, if your fetus has no chance of surviving, you still are required to carry it to term, which means you must give birth to a dead baby, or even worse, one born alive, gasping for breath until they die. The Texas law does not include exceptions for rape, incest, or a fatal fetal diagnosis.

Lauren Hall, one of a dozen women and two doctors suing Texas, was 18 weeks pregnant and had set up a crib and bought clothes for the baby girl she had already named Amelia when scans revealed that the fetus had no skull and an undeveloped brain. A specialist urged her to go out of state, but to tell no one where she was going or why, lest someone report her to a hotline that anti-abortion groups had set up.

Hall said many of her relatives and neighbors considered themselves "pro-life" and believed there was a "loophole" if the fetus had a fatal condition. And many of her friends did not understand that the procedure she obtained at a clinic outside Seattle, dilation and curettage, was the same as an abortion.

"A lot of them are in support of this ban, but they don't understand the scale of it," she said. "They had this very narrow idea of what somebody who seeks an abortion looks like. They think it is somebody who's loose, who doesn't want to take birth control."[54]

It is even worse for mothers who are having problem pregnancies, said Joanna Grossman, a professor at Southern Methodist University's Dedman School of Law. There is no treatment to stop a miscarriage once it has started, and miscarriages can become life-threatening fairly quickly if complications are left untreated. In cases of unviable pregnancies in which fetal cardiac activity can still be detected, treatment to remove the expected miscarriage is considered illegal under Texas's law.

"You worry about the period of time," said Grossman, "when what's going to be a miscarriage, if you let it take a natural course, might cause severe suffering, and/or death to the mother. If you do something to prevent that, you might be in fact performing an illegal abortion."[55]

The lack of clarity accompanying the threat of jail time and six-figure fines for medical professionals has led some hospitals and doctors in the state to deny or delay care for pregnancy complications according to multiple reports. Doctors and experts also worry that patients with pregnancy complications may be too afraid of being accused of inducing an abortion to seek care until it is too late.

Time to Move Forward

Whether in Texas, or in places where women have even fewer rights, or in Afghanistan and parts of Pakistan, where women have no rights at all, we need change to go forward instead of backward. It would be incredible if conservative religious parents would think twice before treating their daughters as second-class citizens or worse. And what if the parents of children with different sexualities and gender fluidity accepted rather than disowned their children? As it is now, these parents are elevating their holy text's ancient understanding of sexuality over both parental love and the findings of current science.

Imagine a world where the legal systems gave equal rights to everyone—rights to education, jobs, and family planning—and where religions no longer perpetuated God as the president of a heterosexual men's club in which at best second-class status and at worst no membership at all was given others. Humanity's hopes for peace, prosperity, justice, and a sustainable future for everyone would be within reach.

Repurposing the Holy Texts Ecologically

Further, not allowing our beliefs to evolve along with our society not only has harmful direct results, but harmful indirect ones as well. It confirms in us the intellectual and emotional habit of clinging to the past—the entire past, not just its positive but also its worst aspects. This affects every facet of our lives and the planet's. And it doesn't just apply to how we treat our children and each other.

We use our own tradition, Christianity, as an example of a faith constituency that has had a huge impact on the ecological crisis. In spite of its many positive actions, Christianity is still falling short in major areas, and there are theological reasons for this.

In the past Christians, especially Protestants, have tended to dive into questions of a personal relationship with God and redemption in the hereafter and to put less emphasis on the relationship of God with the world as a whole. Too often Christianity has been world-denying rather than world-affirming.

The broader Christian tradition, especially among progressive Christians (including progressive Catholics), has done somewhat better. In fact, a theology of nature (the relation between God and the world) has been at the center of the God-and-world debates in the Catholic Church's papal investigations.[56]

If Christianity as a whole had a theology of nature as robust as its theology of redemption, the planet would be in much better shape today. We need to expand our focus.

The Christian tradition has always been about right relationships in all directions—between God, the world, and one another. Isn't it ironic, given such a broad, holistic definition of relationships, that Christians are often the ones pushing a single, individualistic message? Too often, we've truncated Christianity to simply "How's my soul with God?"

Part Two: Religion Comes of Age

Science doesn't allow that. It doesn't let us pull humanity out of the fabric of nature. It asks us to look at human beings against the backdrop of the whole web of life. Interestingly, science's broader message and a broad understanding of the god-world relationship point toward similar conclusions; science and progressive Christian theology are natural and critically important philosophical allies.

Unfortunately, we don't see a real partnership between science and religion at work very often—not in most sermons and Bible studies. More typically, religious people determine what science should have said, or what it should mean, based on their own scriptures and religious beliefs.

Yet surely believers are called to include the transcendent and prophetic dimensions of their faith when they look at the needs of our world. How did such a universal perspective get turned into a focus on individual salvation?

We've also neglected the Jewish and Christian prophetic traditions of challenging the status quo—of asking whether the structures that most people take for granted are just and life-giving, or fall short and should be reconsidered.

Western philosophy has been part of the problem. It has long been obsessed with the question of certainty. Modern philosophers disputed many of Christianity's traditional claims, and so began asking, "What can I be certain of?" The famous father of modern philosophy, René Descartes, answered that the individual can at least be certain that he exists: "I think, therefore I am." That set up a 250-year precedent of striving for an impossible goal: trying to build all thought upon absolutely certain principles. At the same time, Descartes's focus on individual certainty spawned an emphasis on the individual at the expense of the community that has persisted right down to the present day.

The certainty of one's own ideas became the foundation for knowledge. The intelligent individual was a brave soul separate from the world—a brilliant hero who would overcome all challenges through personal internal focus and rational certainty. Emotions and feelings, the body, nature—all these were secondary. That was the theme of much of modern philosophy. As a result, the church bought into this individualistic thinking as well, increasingly emphasizing the importance of personal salvation.

Right now, the church is locked in a struggle between an interconnected approach and the "I-centered" approach. Too many congregations attract believers through messages appealing to individual concerns, desires, and fears: "Come here, and you will enjoy prosperity," and "Come here, and your life/luck will improve," and "Come here, and you'll be saved from eternal damnation."

The teachings of Jesus are better reflected when people work together for the good of all, and become a community. Instead of being fixated on "I," they have a broader sense of the world: a "we" that calls for their participation.

Whatever their faith or nonfaith, people need to join the growing movement of religious thinkers and leaders who are discovering that a more adequate language of god, combined with that of environmental science, can help us decentralize the human self and move the interconnectedness of all things back to the center again, which is a worldview appropriate to an omnipresent god. We need to reflect an ecological worldview in our theology.

The Parable of the Fossil Fuels

There was a time when the use of fossil fuels greatly contributed to the development of our culture and even our species. The energy they gave us made all kinds of technical innovations possible; freed up much of our time by powering inventions that streamlined work inside and outside the home; and allowed us to use that free time to see more of our country and more of the world, as travel by car and plane became affordable to the middle and working classes. Fossil fuels made the world a much smaller, more closely engaged and interconnected place.

But along the way, as we now know, they also made it an ecologically poorer place, and have now made it a gravely threatened one.

If we care for our children, if we are not to sacrifice their future, we must stop clinging to the "sacred" tradition of powering our economic system with oil and coal. Today, there are many alternative sources of energy available. There are also rising ocean levels; cycles of drought, flood, fire, and famine; and increasing mass extinctions. Scientists have confirmed, and responsible world leaders acknowledge, that these modern plagues are caused, directly and indirectly, by global warming. They are a very clear warning. We must do a much better job of making the hard choices that will begin to mitigate the damage that we've already done, and prevent worse disasters in the future.

Today Earth can't regenerate fast enough to keep up with our overfishing the seas, overharvesting the forests, and polluting the waters, land, and air. We must choose to be less comfortable now in order to create a vastly better future for everyone. That's how social evolution works—how change and growth can be a good god's plan for us and for our interconnected world.

It is Time for an "Eco-Evidential Reformation"

The Reverend Michael Dowd, best-selling author and ecotheologian, argues that for the sake of our own survival humanity needs to move from the second era of religious development to the third. To explain, he posits three stages of religious development:

- Era 1: The authority of tribal elders. The elders of antiquity decreed their tribe's concepts of morality and spiritual beliefs, just as they decreed the ordering of daily life.

- Era 2: The authority of scripture. The collective intelligence of the ancient leaders determined which of the myriad of texts that claimed to be divinely inspired would become part of the official canon for a particular religion. That canon and those scriptures then became the unchanging authority for concepts of morality and of God.

- Era 3: The authority of knowledge and scientific evidence, combined with the deepest wisdom of our faith traditions. Today, the global collective intelligence of scientists from a huge variety of religious and secular traditions weighs in on the latest discoveries in physics, biology, psychology, and other disciplines, and collectively arrives at conclusions about what is real and what is most important for our future. This partnership between science and faith can also shed light on aspects of ethics and spirituality. This development is, says Dowd, the "Evidential Reformation." It is what Carl Sagan was getting at when he said, "Science is, at least in part, informed worship."[57]

Many in the world are still stuck in Era 2, elevating their ancient holy texts over the revelations of science. As we discussed in previous chapters, when believers insist that the end-times will come soon or that an omnipotent God is in charge or that only one scripture is true, they are not motivated to make the changes necessary for a sustainable future, and may even oppose them. Furthermore, social ills abound when we hew to ancient understandings of behavior and morality instead of accepting the current knowledge of our evolutionary heritage and its influence over our thoughts and actions.

Science, Religion, and Sacred Stories

The Bottom Line

When scientific reality and ethics conflict with a specific religious dogma, then reality and ethics should win. And the reality is beautiful: It is the basis for the Great Story of our time. Both the truths it has revealed and its myriad of remaining mysteries are endlessly compelling.

Our exponentially growing body of knowledge raises ever more intriguing questions. Again and again, scientific discovery has reframed our cultural imagination about who we are, what the cosmos is, and what our place in it is. In a sense, science can be seen as a theological adventure. Each major discovery is like a rock falling into a pond, sending out ripples that impact the various shores: art, ethics, religion, and our sense of meaning.

Even as our place has been revealed as more minuscule in the grand scheme of everything, our minds are able to glimpse more of reality's mystery and vastness. Truly, finding god as we investigate these grand mysteries is much more awe-inspiring than absurd attempts to cram science into the creation myths of Genesis. Instead of seeking to reinforce speculations about nature that were conceived thousands of years ago, we can celebrate the mysteries that are now opening up in the beautiful, majestic, and ever-expanding cosmos where we make our home. This is not a disenchantment of the world, but a deeper spirituality.

* * *

The Blessing of Pluralism

There is another advantage to moving to an acceptance of the evolving Great Story told by science and religion together. It is the end of tribalism, religious and otherwise. It is happening slowly, in fits and starts. But once we accept that we all share common ancestors and that no one religion or particular secular worldview has a monopoly on truth, there is hope that we can evolve beyond the old habits of in-group and out-group thinking lodged deep in our brains and biochemistry. Transcending in-group loyalties may be the single most important step if humanity as a whole is to respond in time to the global crises—climate change; economic injustice; deadly ethnic, religious, and political conflicts; and the threat of nuclear war—that we have created.

When discussions begin with metaphysics, the differences are sharp. But when we begin with spiritual practice and ethical conviction, we discover significant common ground.

We all pray in some sense—even those of us who are atheists, since prayer can be a hope, assurance, or request voiced to ourselves as well as to god. We all look for deeper meaning. We all have rituals that anchor our lives, which we invest with special significance and honor in special ways. We all carry out actions we think work for our own good and the good of those around us. There is much we can learn from each other's practices and experiences—awe and wonder, mindfulness and equanimity—even when we disagree about the specifics of religion and theology. We can be inspired by the spiritual generosity, altruism, and compassion of those whose beliefs differ from our own.

Why Seek Common Ground Between Atheists and Believers?

This is what we have been advocating ever since Chapter 1, when we suggested expanded definitions of "sacred" and "spirituality" to encompass both secular and religious worldviews. Why is this so important?

- First and foremost, because, although we may believe we are right, we can't decisively know that we are.

- Second, because significant common ground really does exist between theists and atheists. It is tragic when disputes over beliefs make it seem as if we inhabit different planets. We inhabit one planet, we all belong here, and if we can't learn together to protect and sustain it and each other, we're all in trouble.

- Third, because even if theists are wrong and there is no god, many of the values that are tied up with belief in god are still true. In this case, instead of being based on an actual god, theistic beliefs would be based on the evolutionary emergence of *the idea of God* as a human construct. Obviously for theists, conceiving god as an emergent and purely human construct—a useful fiction, in other words—would be much less compelling than the god that they (and one of us) believe in. But humans are not theists or nontheists first. First of all, we are human beings, and the common values that bind us and our fellow human beings together across the "God divide" are more important than the divide itself.

There is one more aspect of this debate to consider, and it is extremely important for the future of faith. Suppose that there *is* a god. Then, as the previous chapters have demonstrated, god must be omnipresent—present everywhere, at all times past and present, including with every creature, at every moment, in every era.

If there is a god, all of us, believers and nonbelievers, are continually encountering god, whether we call our moments of deep-seated peace, joy, love, and awe an experience of the divine or something else. Humans describe their most meaningful and profound experiences in different ways, depending on time, place, religion, and culture. If you grew up in the Swat Valley of Pakistan, you will have a completely different way of expressing these experiences than if you grew up in Chicago. But if the god hypothesis is right, all of us, including atheists, are experiencing god, whether we call what we experience god or not.

Therefore, we need not focus on our neighbors' differing beliefs, unless their beliefs cause them to act in unethical ways. Rather, we can focus on enhancing our interconnectedness and the common good. This is immensely liberating.

Pluralism Is Imperative

It also means pluralism is a mandate. Those who damn every theology but their own are idolizing their theology more than worshiping their god. Where is their faith that their god can work through a variety of views?

Each of the world's religions has rich traditions and different expertise to draw upon: Buddhist meditation, Hindu pluralism, Jewish ethical rigor and love of justice, Christian grace and forgiveness, Muslim stress on the glory and compassion of God, indigenous religions' recognition of the sacredness of the earth . . . The more accounts there are of the divine, the less the adherents of any one of them one should be certain their own is the only truth. The more varied and multiple religions are, the less dogmatic they should be.

We need to develop the humility that grows from the soil of a religiously plural world. Our lives are so much richer when we move beyond certainty and absolutism and open ourselves up to insights and wisdom from other spiritual traditions, and from the realities we learn from science.

Admittedly, an embrace of pluralism does not sit well with the most conservative believers of a particular faith. Nevertheless, they are at their best when they embrace the spiritual practices that give them strength, yet also practice an openness that allows them to work with adherents of other faiths for the well-being of all—in this way increasing compassion, justice, and peace, and conserving our biosphere so that future generations can thrive.

The Benefits of Pluralism: Examples

We close this chapter with examples of the positive experiences that are possible when pluralism is embraced rather than feared, by revisiting two of the people we introduced in Chapter 8.

Meryem, Revisited

Meryem is despondent about a recent political flare-up between the campus Jewish and Muslim clubs, groups that had formerly held friendship events together. She decides to contact Rachel, a Jewish student she likes who had once invited her to a Shabbat service.

Given the current conflict, Rachel is surprised that Meryem has chosen this time to accept her Shabbat invitation, but she obliges. They attend her temple that Friday night.

As the worship progresses, Meryem unexpectedly finds herself deeply moved. The fact that the rabbi is a woman, and a very gifted one at that, is immensely liberating. Meryem has never experienced mixed worship led by a woman before. She is also struck by how much the rabbi's chanting of the Torah reminds her of her own imam's chanting of the Qur'an, and she is overcome by the feeling of reverence that it invokes. The temple's tranquil, uplifting environment heightens her sense of spiritual awe. Gradually Meryem's brooding about the campus conflict evaporates.

Rachel, in turn, finds the Shabbat service more meaningful and profound than usual because she senses how deeply Meryem is moved by it. They may speak of god as "Elohim" or as "Allah," but somehow the same god is present to them both.

As they are leaving, Meryem tells Rachel that she had initiated the visit to try to reduce some of the tension between their groups in some small way. But, she says, she had no idea that she would find the ceremony so spiritually moving. As they hug each other, they each feel deeply that at some level they are truly sisters, sisters who share the same god.

Matthew, Revisited

Matthew's marriage is in trouble, and he and his wife have decided to take separate vacations to calm down and gain objectivity. They plan to begin joint marriage counseling when they return, but each sadly wonders if their marriage is beyond repair. Matthew decides on a cycling trip through southern France with his French friend Théo, who is Catholic.

Sensing that Matthew is in a dark place, Théo makes sure their bike route passes a particular little country chapel that he loves—a shrine in honor of an ancient nun's vision of the Virgin Mary. He suggests they take a break there to enjoy the sacred tranquility of the setting, and Matthew readily agrees.

When Théo kneels in front of the chapel's altar and closes his eyes, Matthew does likewise. The spirit of the place is almost palpable, and suddenly Matthew finds himself having an overwhelming experience of a feminine divine. It fits no category of God that he has ever before encountered—his Protestant God has always been decidedly male, and the Virgin Mary of Catholicism is viewed as suspect in his tradition.

Completely overcome, Matthew begins to weep. Théo stays next to him as a comforting presence until Matthew is able to move again. At that point, their knees creaky from kneeling so long, they stroll around the chapel gardens for another forty minutes as Théo recounts to Matthew the story of the nun's encounter with the Virgin. When they continue on their way, Matthew feels drained but profoundly refreshed.

He still doubts whether he and his wife will be able to save their marriage when they return from their respective vacations. In spite of that, he is at peace, buoyed by the feeling that this incredible experience of the feminine divine will sustain him during the difficulties they will face in the next stages of their relationship.

* * *

Part Two: Religion Comes of Age

We are blessed to be alive today. We are participants in a saga that embraces the grandeur of our cosmos and the challenges and joys of our existence; and we are conscious of this fact in ways that our ancestors were not able to experience. We have a vast array of awe-inspiring knowledge at our fingertips.

We no longer need to fear what we don't understand, or to attribute disasters to an angry God who must be appeased. Equally, we no longer need to fear "the other" because they look or believe differently from us. Instead, we can now enjoy a wide diversity of wisdom, not only from science and other branches of advanced human knowledge, but also from the world's many faiths, as we attempt to live into our deepest ideals, truths, and compassion.

The challenges we face are great, but we can take comfort in the knowledge that we are all in this together—no single religion, country, technology, or individual is responsible for overcoming all of the difficulties, and no one person, people, faith, or discipline can do it alone. If we all do our part, we can protect and conserve much of this lovely planet with which we've been entrusted, and together create an enlightened future for our children and our children's children. This is truly a Great Story—one we can all embrace.

12

Our Sacred Story: Two Visions

HUMANITY HAS BEEN SEEKING the transcendent for all of recorded history. Our ancient ancestors did so based upon the worldviews of their time, combined with their sense of awe and the beliefs and values that they held. They created their metaphysics as best as they could, given their rudimentary understanding of the laws of nature, with no knowledge of the birth of the universe or the origins of life. At some point, long ago, a few of our ancestors began to understand the transcendent as a single Almighty God who created and ruled over everything. This idea spread and took hold in many of the world's religions. It still dominates many people's concepts of transcendence today.

Now, however, we know a tremendous amount about how creation actually happened and how nature works. This book has summarized much of what humanity has learned. We can examine the ancient God language we've inherited to see how it ties in with what we now know to be reality.

Many have looked at the evidence of our cosmic creation and exclaimed, "Ha, we've solved the question of God! God is just a human invention, a socially produced construct like our cultures or our systems of commerce." To come of age, to embrace the world of science, they say, requires one to leave religion behind as an illusion from the past, a fantasy realm from the childhood of our species.

We believe that this blanket dismissal shortchanges human yearnings for the transcendent. It represents a kind of either/or thinking that actually obscures rather than unveils the deeper nature of reality. Beyond the simplistic either/or dichotomy lie profound connections between science, spirituality, and yes, even religion.

Each person or group adopts a particular narrative, a story they tell about how these two fundamental features of human existence are related. If your narrative presupposes that science and religion are at war, you are unlikely to discover areas where the two can supplement each other and work as allies. If the story you tell has a place for science and spirituality to cross-fertilize, you'll be able to experience the awe, wonder, reverence, even knowledge and ethical insight, that arise at the areas where the scientific quest and the religious quest overlap.

To give you a sense of how this can work, we'd like to share the spiritual narratives that each of us as authors has adopted. We begin with our two different accounts of how we find meaning, followed by a brief summary of how we each describe the sacred story of our creation, interweaving Pearce's secular worldview with Clayton's panentheistic worldview. Though they differ in important ways, both of our worldviews share a common set of core values, best summarized perhaps by the principle that all people (no matter what religious or secular beliefs they hold) have a responsibility to aim for a life that is personally fulfilling and at the same time contributes to the greater good for *everyone*, including efforts to protect the beautiful biosphere that humanity's actions have placed at risk. We also share the belief that the best way to reach this goal is to be a part of communities that encourage and support each other in these endeavors.

- Clayton: Like other panentheists, I believe in a deeper dimension of reality that many call the divine. Rather than thinking of God as above and separate from the world around us, however, I conceive the divine as deeply interfused with life and the cosmos. The scientific and spiritual quests are two complementary dimensions of what it means to be human. From this starting point, cosmic, biological, cultural, and personal evolution become interconnected parts of a continual process of emergence—an adventure of both mind and spirit.

  Seen in this way, the natural world is more than a two-dimensional flatland in which microphysical forces are the sole reality and human consciousness is just a byproduct of "wires and chemicals." Instead, we witness a continual emergence of novelty: from complex physical forces to emergent chemical structures to simple life-forms to diverse ecosystems to new forms of human awareness to the

Our Sacred Story: Two Visions

conscious, value-filled lives that we know as persons. How could our origin story not be both scientific and spiritual, interwoven together in our very nature?

The more science teaches us about evolution, the better we understand ourselves and our capacities to do harm or to bring about good. Working together, science and spirituality give rise to the human experiences of wonder, awe, reverence, self-transcendence, moral striving, and feeling at home in the universe. Together they affirm that here, in this universe and on this planet, something of cosmic significance is at work.

Although I am a theist, there are many claims in the classical creeds and the traditional theology texts that I cannot affirm. I do not believe in an omnipotent God, one who sets aside natural laws to work literal miracles in the world. I view the world as permeated by a divine presence; all things exist within that presence, and it is present within all living beings. Panentheists affirm a divine lure on individuals and on evolving life as a whole, drawing us toward compassion, love, justice, and interconnection. We share this common commitment in different forms, even though we are Jews, Christians, Muslims, Hindus, Buddhists, Taoists, and religiously unaffiliated persons.[58]

We view humanity and all of nature as involved in a project of co-creation with the divine, an all-pervading indwelling that enfolds life and consciousness, culture and value, nature and civilization. However you may conceive "god" or "God," this word surely connotes a source and a presence far bigger than ourselves—something so comprehensive that it spans the entire cosmos, from alpha to omega. To affirm that god exists is to affirm an omnipresent reality of infinite depth, infinite breadth, infinite goodness. It is also to accept the invitation to participate with the divine in the creation of value here and now and into the future.

The word "god" can never be self-contained; it can never turn inward on itself, never be defined in abstraction from the sum total of reality as we are coming to know it. God language should expand what our minds and hearts can take in, helping us to perceive a multidimensional world where value, beauty, and interconnectedness become central to our lives—a world where we strive to know what is beneficial and to do what is good.

- Pearce: Any thoughtful person who is unable to believe in God or god must construct meaning in ways that are different from those who believe in Something More. Fortunately, many humanists, atheists, and agnostics have been considering these questions for centuries now, so there is plenty of help for those who are grappling with these issues.

    As a humanist, I don't deny that the panentheist vision that Philip describes (above and also below, in "Our Sacred Story Revisited") is the more appealing and inspiring vision for ultimate meaning. Further, much in our book supports the possibility of panentheism, and I would love to feel there is "an omnipresent reality of infinite goodness at the core of the universe" that gently influences us and the rest of creation. Most of the time, however, I am unable to believe that there is, given that so much suffering and injustice is inflicted by human cultural and religious beliefs and actions. So, for me, natural processes seem to better explain the slow, bumpy progress that the human race has made in terms of consciousness, ethics, justice, and a concern for our biosphere.

    Like most humanists, I am continually awed by the majesty and mysteries of the universe and the wild extravagance of nature. I am especially grateful to be living in an era when human knowledge has advanced far enough for us to realize that, in a sense, the universe is using us, its creations, to understand itself. It is breathtaking when you think about it. Far from feeling "two-dimensional" and mechanistic, these opportunities and experiences are more than rich enough to fulfill my need for meaning, awe, and transcendence—as they are for most of the humanists, atheists, and agnostics I know.

    Our desire to make the most of the one life we have causes us to seek the same things as most people—career satisfaction, love, spiritually sustaining practices, fun, friendship, thankfulness, and so on. This desire also leads us to attempt to make a positive difference in collaboration with others with similar goals. Our mortality motivates us to prioritize goals that will make the world a better place, since this is the only world we have, and it is precious.

    For secularists in the direst straits, that desire may manifest itself as simply striving to reduce their own suffering and that of those around them. Others with more resources often work for social justice and a sustainable world. Personally, I have long concentrated much of my writing and activism on the areas that I founds most damaging in the religion in which I was raised. After so much progress, it is been dismaying to see the backlash return in so many ways.

Our realization that *this life is our ultimate purpose* motivates us to persevere. In contrast, those who have a traditional religious faith in immortality tend to devalue our finite mortal lives as a lower form of being. Their main motivation is to make sure they, their loved ones, and others they meet achieve a blissful eternity by accepting their belief system. Such a belief system provides less motivation to work for the common good, since this life is only an inferior, temporary waystation.

This unfortunate result often seems to hold for those who claim that their faith is the only one true faith. But it doesn't hold as often for the many questioning people who are more toward the middle of the belief spectrum—those who hold their religious beliefs with humility and value pluralism. I am grateful for the many people of faith who occupy this middle place on the belief spectrum. They are kindred spirits.

* * *

Intertwining the Visions

Building on these two narratives, we now invite you to consider two examples of how god language can supplement science. In each case, we first state the Story of Creation from a naturalistic point of view, and then imagine how panentheists might supplement the naturalist account to include the idea of an all-pervading divine presence.

1. In the Beginning, our particular universe exploded into being.
   Panentheists add: At that time, there was a Ground of All Things that held infinite, unlimited possibilities. In the beginning, this ground was pure potentiality, holding unrealized creativity that would rapidly emerge. From the beginning, this divine ground has been responsive to evolving reality in all its forms, participating in and drawing out its emerging complexity and deeper value.

2. As time continued, more and more potential things became actual. The interactions of matter and energy produced chemical compounds, and they in turn produced living cells. More and more complex organisms emerged over time, all interconnected. As living systems became

more complex, so too did their capacity for inner experience: for awareness, feeling, mental representations, and social learning; and eventually for self-consciousness, imagination, rational reflection, the pursuit of beauty, and an awakening to the transcendent.

The way the world is at any given instant determines what it can become in the next. The world, in that respect, is much like us: If you hadn't trained so hard, you couldn't have completed the marathon. Your college degree helped you get your first job. Working on your current relationships will give you deeper relationships in the future.

Panentheists add a draw toward goodness: Everything that exists co-creates the future and influences the next set of outcomes. Integral to this co-creation is a divine lure toward the good. This lure does not force itself miraculously from outside the system, but permeates all that is. It helps us understand the interconnectedness of everything and the evolutionary influences that favor cooperation and care. It works through natural causes: through our friends, relatives, and leaders at their best; through great music, art, and literature; through the moral character we build when we make good choices; and through all that is good in creation.

The all-encompassing, indwelling divine has been growing in experience and complexity as well—in response to and in interrelation with creation. This Ground of All Things can be understood as Good, rather than morally neutral. As cosmic evolution proceeds, the divine life and sacred awareness continue to grow and expand. This can be seen as reciprocal: the divine is continuously gaining new experiences from interaction with everything that is, and feeding those experiences back as new pulls toward novelty, creativity, and compassion.

As you see, these two visions are not identical, but they are complementary. The panentheistic god does not negate natural laws and patterns or break into natural systems from outside; instead, the god language supplements the best scientific accounts. For some, a not-less-than-personal divine presence undergirds cosmic evolution, luring it toward goodness. For others, these notions go too far; a more thoroughgoing naturalistic account is preferable.

Our Sacred Story: Two Visions

Embracing the Discoveries of Science

In contrast to the complementarity of these two visions, our ancient ancestors, with their more limited knowledge, created images of God and the universe that were often tribal, absolutist, and unchanging. But history shows us that true wisdom increases when it is informed by knowledge. By contrast, nothing moves forward when we do not allow current knowledge to inform past wisdom: not science, not human understanding, and especially not the common good.

That's why we should resist the temptation to use God as an explanation for what we haven't yet explained—as a kind of "God of the gaps." Instead, we continue to subject the unknown to critical reflection and further research. We no longer resort to God to fill in the holes in the ongoing pursuit of knowledge. And when new discoveries about the universe, life, and human existence undercut previously held beliefs, we rejoice in the adventure of learning and the ongoing progress toward greater insight.

As Neil deGrasse Tyson illustrates in his lecture during a Science Network conference in November 2006, when Sir Isaac Newton couldn't explain why the elliptical orbits of the planets around the sun remained stable, based on his two-body gravitational equations, he attributed the stability to God. Historians of science often conjecture that if Newton had not been convinced that God was stabilizing the planetary orbits, he would have kept searching and likely would have discovered the calculus necessary to explain the phenomenon. It certainly would not have required a big leap for his brilliant mind. But as soon as he attributed the unknown to God, the search for a scientific reason stopped. If the brilliant Sir Isaac Newton said that God was the only possible explanation, others would hardly question his wisdom. It took another century before a talented scientist arose—Pierre-Simon Laplace—who dared to question Newton's conclusion and went on to solve the problem. When Napoleon asked Laplace where God was in his new theory, he is said to have replied, "Sir, I have no need of that hypothesis."[59]

Today scientists are diving into the major mysteries of the natural world with wonder and enthusiasm. In the process, they are making ever more exciting discoveries. Some of the discoveries reduce the plausibility of traditional theological accounts of who God is and how God acts in the world. Confronted with new tensions, people can put up walls and insulate their religious beliefs more and more carefully from the advance of science. Or they can welcome the new insights with the enthusiasm expressed by the philanthropist Sir John Templeton in his well-known maxim: "How little we know, how eager to learn."

As we saw in the previous section, there are ways of being religious and understanding god that are not undercut by the ongoing expansion of human knowledge. Both scientists and religious persons, both naturalists and theists, have need of the virtue of intellectual humility. After all, at the horizons of our quest for understanding lies mystery. Whether theists or atheists, we can learn to greet the mysteries around us and the mysteries within us with awe and wonder. Mystery will always confront us—as we stare out into the heavens, as we reflect on the birth of a child or the birth of the universe, as we contemplate our own death and what might come afterward.

Enhanced Human Understanding

In the same vein, we no longer attribute our all-too-human failings to demonic activity or to a lack of trust in God, nor do we beat ourselves up for feeling flashes of lust, greed, selfishness, and other undesirable impulses. Rather, we accept the fact that all of us share an evolutionary heritage that causes conflicting desires. This understanding frees us to devise more constructive methods of dealing with inappropriate desires and actions, both individually and collectively. Furthermore, we value the rich diversity and variety in nature, leaving behind old hierarchies that privileged males over females, heterosexuals over homosexuals, one race or caste over another, and so on, to the detriment of us all. Traditional wisdom informed by current scientific understanding of human behavior, far from making us less moral and less reverent toward things of the spirit, can actually assist us in our ethical and spiritual quest. Bringing contemporary science and traditional wisdom together also increases our compassion toward others by making us aware that we all share the same hopes and struggles.

Better Serving the Common Good

As we've learned from nature, "survival of the fittest" most often means "survival of the most cooperative." It is now overwhelmingly clear that if our future generations and those of Earth's other species are to survive, we *must* cooperate more effectively to save the exquisite biosphere that sustains us all. It is not a religious virtue to deny the increasing human-caused threats to our future that science has so clearly illuminated. Rather, it is suicide. If we continue on our present path, we will become the agents of our own extinction, joining the myriad of other plant and animal species that no longer exist because of our actions.

The interconnectedness at the core of the cosmos means we are all members of the same tribe. Acknowledging this fact makes us better able to take on the challenges that face us. But we must make this acknowledgment without undercutting that which most inspires us—the sense of transcendence that humanity has traditionally found in religion.

Reuniting Mystery and Knowledge

For most of human history, mystery and knowledge have existed side by side, complementary and mutually enhancing. Reflection on what seemed inexplicable eventually produced explanations—new knowledge—and the advance of knowledge inevitably revealed new mysteries. Over the past few decades, however, some people have lost track of that symmetrical relationship. Many began to view knowledge and mystery as antagonistic. Some scientists and some religious people decided that explanation is a zero-sum game: a gain for science is a loss for religion, and vice versa.

This book has been written in service of a different and, we think, greater vision: the dream that our species may again rediscover the mutually supportive relationship between knowledge and mystery. This vision is exactly the opposite of the zero-sum viewpoint. Mystery continually inspires science, and scientific seeking leads to new knowledge—without in any way eclipsing the mysteries that still remain. With every great increase in what we know, the unknown grows as well. You can glory in the power of the human intellect and the progressive evolution of our species, while pondering the mystery of human existence, life and death. And you can use the name "god," or other traditionally religious terms, to identify the Great Mystery that lies at least partially beyond the boundaries of knowledge, not in order to fix limits on the quest for knowledge, but in order to spur it to ever-greater advances.

We continue to be struck by the sense of a something greater beyond us, a transcendent something that we can never fully grasp with our minds. Many of us have experienced this transcendence, atheist and believer alike.

Think about the deepest moments of mystery, awe, and wonder—the times when we are conscious of the sheer givenness and grandeur of the cosmos and whatever is behind it. Think of the moment when addicts give up control of their lives to something ineffable, something they can't describe, and gradually their addiction loses its grip. Or the moment when a surpassing love and awareness for all of those around us, and for creation itself, overwhelms us.

This thing that gives meaning, that is the ground of goodness and compassion, and that undergirds the existence and order of the world around us—this thing that is as complex as all the complexity in the universe, that doesn't preprogram everything from the outset, but leaves an open end to the future, an invitation to co-create—this is the great mystery that some call "God," others call "god," and almost all of us (secular and religious alike) call "the Sacred."

A Relationship with Transcendence

What kind of communion can we have with this kind of Sacredness? While their concepts of God may have been problematic, our ancestors were definitely experienced at communing with the sacred. Their best practices continue to work well, for they were based on the responses humans have always had when they've experienced the ineffable.

Prayer continues to be an important practice for many. Those who no longer find the term "god" helpful can still pray: to the interconnected Universe, to Love, or to Something Bigger. They can even talk to the future self they want to become.

We have mentioned other practices: living ethically; studying creation through science; exploring theology; practicing meditation, silence, or centering; seeking community; becoming conscious of the sacred in our fellow humans, in nature, in music, a great novel, or other art.

Therapy can be extremely helpful for achieving emotional wellness, self-knowledge, and the wherewithal to remain open to the sacred. Then there are the activist practices: striving for peace and justice, defending the poor and oppressed.

All of these help us stay in communion with goodness and the sacred.

Many will continue to perform these practices in the context of their traditional religion, even while more and more people are performing them in secular settings. Whatever our religious or secular location, however, our responses to the sacred must be clothed in a deep humility—an acknowledgement that no one religion can have a monopoly on truth, and that the best paths to the spiritual will vary from person to person, depending on differences in temperament, culture, and age, or the religion or philosophy that each finds most compelling. Finding this core that draws us toward good is a lifelong process: moments of transcendence regularly intermingled with uncertainties, triumphs with failures, joys with sorrows—together with all the other moments that we encounter along the way.

13

Conclusion
Now What?

WHAT DO WE DO with what we now know? The last 75 years have been a time of incredible discovery. Our knowledge has literally grown by light-years. It is time to let the groundbreaking discoveries of our era reanimate the most fundamental questions of our spiritual life.

> Why am I here?
> What is my place in the universe?
> Why are we the way we are?
> Is there an ultimate goal or purpose to life?

When we use knowledge to inform our religions and communities, discarding harmful moral codes and dated concepts, we re-engage the deepest wisdom of our traditions. Rather than relying on a supernatural Father to fix the messes we've made, we acknowledge that we are truly the authors of our destiny. This allows us to face the huge challenges of our age with clarity and courage.

Consider: In 1800, at the dawn of the Industrial Revolution, there were roughly a billion people on the planet. The waters were teeming with fish, and the skies with birds. Forests, prairies, and wetlands thrived. And it was very good.

In the twenty-two decades since then, the human population has expanded to eight billion people, and we've caused the mass extinction of a myriad of plant and animal species. Throughout the world our species has destroyed forests, paved over prairies, drained wetlands, and severely compromised fisheries. The pollution we've dumped into our lands, oceans, and air will have lasting negative repercussions. We've altered the trajectory of our future. It is even possible that, much like the vanished Easter Islanders, we will be the agents of our extinction. Clearly, we've had a lapse of wisdom.

The Glaring Environmental Divide

For those people whose ethics and/or spirituality engages them with the world and its betterment, global climate change is deeply concerning. But for many conservative religious persons in different cultures, including conservative evangelicals and fundamentalists in North America, the opposite is true. Religious opinions, of course, are also strongly tied to political partisanship, which emerges as a crucial factor in explaining differing views on the environment and global warming. Democrats, and independents who lean toward the Democratic Party, are far more likely than Republicans and those who lean Republican to say that climate change is an extremely or very serious problem. A November 17, 2022, Pew Report had 83 percent of Democrats ranking climate change as "extremely high" or "very high" on their list of concerns, compared with 25 percent of Republicans, a huge gap that also reflects many apparent differences in views among religious groups. Significantly, 68 percent of religious "nones" say stricter environmental laws and regulations would be worth whatever they cost.

In contrast, 66 percent of white evangelicals believe it is extremely or very likely that the U.S. will overreact to global climate change by creating too many unnecessary environmental regulations, causing a gradual loss of individual freedoms in the next decades—regulations that many of them plan to fight.[60]

They ignore the fact that, when it comes to the global climate crisis, clinging to our traditional ways will be far more than expensive—it will be catastrophic. Their misguided belief is dangerous. It flies in the face of the realities of science and knowledge. Freed from superstition, science allows us to participate in our own salvation along with that of the rest of this beautiful but damaged world.

Conclusion

A Time to Act

In this book we have suggested ways to update the ancient wisdom of the holy books with the grand and meaningful creation story that we now know to be true. It is a story that encompasses everything from the birth of our universe 13.8 billion years ago, up through the latest revelations of quantum physics and cellular biology—a saga that embraces the challenges and joys of our existence, the values that orient us, and our stumbling attempts to live up to our deepest ideals. What we've called the Great Story inspires us to participate with knowledge *and* wisdom, so that not just humanity, but all of creation can thrive.

It took billions of years of cosmic evolution to create humanity and the fragile world of which we are a part. Now our quest for prosperity has brought us to a critical juncture in space and time. The environmental devastation we have caused is the greatest threat to our children's future and the future of all of Earth's species. The great task of repairing that damage and saving the future will require faith as well as knowledge, from all of us, including those of us who no longer draw our sense of life's sacredness from the stories and practices of traditional religion. We, too, will need to bring a sustaining wisdom and sense of awe to the task, even though belief in a literal God the Father is no longer there for us. But the interconnection of faith, wisdom, knowledge, and awe still remains.

In this interconnection, we sense incredible openings (to use traditional religious language) for prayer, for belonging, for worship, and for seeing the sacred in the world around us. In fact, the amazing thing is that one can now think such thoughts without needing to rely on traditional religious language—or at least not on its traditional, literal meanings. Each of these openings is offered to us by contemporary physics and the study of nature.

Community Is Still Key

For much of human history, our religions have been among the most effective agents for moving us to loyalty, trust, self-sacrifice, and other cooperative behaviors. Given the major challenges that face us, including the polarizing effect of social media, we desperately, more than ever, need effective communities.

Conclusion

Many people are looking for a community of belief that fits in with the major shifts in our understanding of science and the sacred, but have difficulty finding one. They'd like a community that addresses their need for friendship and fun, and their wish to become a better person, and that also inspires a desire to work together to make the world a better place.

As traditional churches and other old forms of religion are receding, newer groups on the cutting edge of today's paradigms are beginning to discover what works for us now. Many of these newly emerging forms of community and spiritual practice (some secular, some religious) are still in their first or middle stages, not yet fully formed. Others are already going strong.

There are more examples than we could possibly list—a wealth of associations that represent vastly different forms and practices that purpose-driven communities can take. In a book written for such a broad readership, all that we can do is to strongly encourage our readers to explore the kinds of intentional communities around them that match their interests, address their longings, and help them find spiritual meaning and purpose in a complex and often confusing world. And if you have been exploring, and still haven't found what you're looking for, we encourage you to keep seeking.

If we heed the impulse that is calling us to protect and conserve the earth we've inherited, then our children and their children's children will continue to enjoy the wonder and majesty of the sacred gifts that we have been given. Our descendants may not realize how close we came to destroying their legacy before we saved it. But at the very least, they will realize the value of their healthy planet and continue to expand the enlightened knowledge of it that we bequeathed to them. Bathed in eternal mystery and sustained by the spiritual sense of the interconnection of all things, may they enjoy the kinds of discoveries that we can only dream about.

Appendix A

Creative Emergence or Intelligent Design?

When the ancient biblical authors observed the magnificent heavenly bodies and earthly creatures, they assumed that all of it must have been created at one time by a powerful, intelligent divinity. They did not have the ability to see the complex internal structures that make up Earth's species, nor were they privy to the evidence that Earth's flora and fauna arose over billions of years through the process of evolution. But they did understand the spirit and impulse toward science—knowledge—as the human spark, just as they understood the impulse toward creation and being as divine.

Today we are incredibly privileged to know so much more about the patterns of nature and the steps by which life evolved. This knowledge is an occasion for thankfulness with awe. Knowing what we know, it is difficult to accept the Creationist or intelligent-design explanation for the forms of being. Yet it need not be difficult to accept the divinity of being itself—the idea that being is something more than its forms. Science does not prove the nonexistence of God; it only changes the way in which believers talk about God's involvement in the creation process.

Appendix A

Fighting Ignorance with Facts Is Not Enough

Scientists are often preoccupied with their research and tend to pay little attention to what the general public believes. They *do* care that the textbooks present basic science accurately, but they don't bring the same fervor to the battle between facts and faith that supporters of Intelligent Design and Creationism do.

When serious scientists debate Creationists, they cite a wealth of empirical evidence and well-proven theories. But rational arguments alone cannot persuade people to abandon fear and prejudice. Intellect cannot argue with feelings. There has to be an outreach from the heart as well as the mind. Too often, evolutionary scientists and the rest of us who write about evolutionary biology leave out the heartfelt wonder, awe, and gratitude we feel for the marvelous process that over millennia produced our world and ourselves—even though we feel these emotions as strongly as any believer in the seven-day creation described in Genesis. And many of us feel that god *is* involved with the process in some way.

If god didn't do all the designing at the very outset, what then? What if god was not the designer of specific beings but instead, supremely, the ground of being, the will to novelty, the source of creativity, the lure toward goodness? What if evolution is the world creating itself in response to a divine call? Such a god would fit far better with modern astronomy and biology—with the heavens and earth as we know them.

Below we consider certain powerful myths about the theory of evolution—myths that are much less compelling once they are examined more closely.

Myth 1: Belief in evolution requires denying the existence of God

The history of evolution contradicts the Genesis account of creation. Therefore, many Intelligent Design supporters and Creationists believe that people who accept and affirm evolution will inevitably lose their faith.

Some people do lose their faith or become more agnostic when they understand the process by which life evolves on this planet, *especially* if they've been taught that the biblical creation stories must be taken literally.

On the other hand, many evolutionists are religious believers—believers who recognize that Genesis was never meant to serve as a science textbook. Rather, they revere it as a collection of ancient but profound stories about why we are here, the human condition, and humanity's relationship with god.

Myth 2: Evolution leads to atheism, which in turn produces evil and depraved behavior

The all-too-common claim that atheism destroys civil society is false. Sociologist Phil Zuckerman in his book *Society Without God* notes that the least religious of the world's nations, Denmark and Sweden, are filled with residents who score at the very top of ethics and happiness indexes:

> Their healthy societies boast some of the lowest rates of violent crime in the world (along with some of the lowest levels of corruption), excellent educational systems, strong economies, well-supported arts, free health care, egalitarian social policies, outstanding bike paths, and great beer.[61]

And in his 2009 book *Good Without God: What a Billion Nonreligious People Do Believe*, Harvard's humanist chaplain, Greg Epstein, describes the many millions of secular humanists who have a "positive belief in tolerance, community, morality, and good" and act accordingly, in spite of their not believing in a higher being.[62]

It is wrong to vilify those who do not hold a belief in God. Most of them have come to the same moral conclusions and live the same decent and mindful, caring life as most believers. In fact, many atheists are doing selfless, heroic work in the most dangerous parts of the world (often with nonprofits such as Doctors Without Borders). They would be candidates for sainthood if they were believers.

Myth 3: Evolution "is just a theory." Schools should be required to also teach other theories, such as Intelligent Design

There is a widespread misunderstanding of the word *theory* in science. In common usage, when you say you have a theory about something, you mean a guess or a hunch. The scientific definition of a theory is completely different. In order to reach the level of theory in science, a hypothesis—an educated guess or hunch—must have had its predictions verified, must be strongly supported by factual evidence, and must be testable and capable of

Appendix A

being proved true or false. Darwin's theory of evolution has stood this test, as fresh discoveries have challenged and ultimately strengthened it.

How a Theory Works: Punctuated Equilibrium

In the mid-twentieth century, based on the discovery of more and more fossils, scientists began realizing that during certain prehistoric eras, many species had appeared at the same time. Since Darwin's original theory of evolution assumed that all species emerged gradually over long periods of time, these new discoveries shook the scientific world. Headlines like "Is Darwinism Dead?" began proliferating. But by the 1970s, further research had explained this phenomenon, now known as punctuated equilibrium.

Scientists have found that most species exhibit little net evolutionary change for most of their history, as long as their environment remains fairly constant. But in certain periods there have been massive and relatively rapid evolutionary changes. These periods often coincided with major environmental pressures—for example from drastic weather changes, earthquakes, volcanic activity, comet strikes, and so on. Rapid changes can also occur when a new positive mutation emerges in a species, which begins to thrive and places new pressures on other species. Note: "Rapid" by evolutionary standards is millions, rather than billions, of years.

Thus, evolution often proceeded in spurts (over multimillions of years), rather than gradually over the 3.5 to 4 billion years since single-celled life first appeared, as Darwin originally hypothesized. Punctuated equilibrium did not disprove evolution, but instead gave us a better understanding of how evolution works. Some of Darwin's assumptions about the process were false, and they have been corrected over time as human knowledge has grown.

When Darwin first postulated the mechanisms of variation and selection, based on his extensive observations of species, the structure and even existence of DNA was unknown. Genes and their role in evolution were discovered only after Darwin's death. That's what happens in science: Theories get refined over time, as more and more evidence accumulates.

Theories must also be able to make predictions, and the predictions have to be testable. For example, evolutionary biologists and paleontologists have made thousands of predictions about what kinds of fossils will be found to fill in various evolutionary gaps in the existing records, based on how evolution works. They can also make predictions about what particular DNA segments these missing links are likely to include. Over and over, discoveries of new fossils have fulfilled these predictions, providing more evidence for the truth of evolutionary theory even as it modifies and advances it.

The Rich DNA and Fossil Record of Transitional Species

Many Creationists and defenders of Intelligent Design we've spoken with continue to ignore all the transitional fossils that have been discovered since the 1950s. They will make statements such as, "Archaeopteryx still has no expected transitional fossils on either side of its appearance, and it is a critical piece in the assumption that birds are descended from certain dinosaurs."[63]

Such statements are a puzzle, since even Wikipedia has a section on the evolution of birds, listing many of the transitional fossils from theropod dinosaurs to current birds and reptiles.[64] In fact, some of the most primitive birds today, like the flightless emus of Australia, still have characteristics left over from Archeopteryx and other dinosaur ancestors, such as the claw at the tip of their wings, as coauthor C.S. Pearce has seen.

When Pearce was writing articles and books for the San Diego Zoo in the 1990s, she became acquainted with many of the thousands of animals and plants there, and was particularly fond of an emu named Daphne. (Part of Daphne's charm was his name: Turns out it is hard even for zookeepers to determine an emu's sex.)

Daphne let Pearce lift up his stubby little wings to examine his pterodactyl-like wing claws, and Pearce returned the favor by letting Daphne mouth her shiny wedding ring—unlike ostrich beaks, which are very sharp and hooked, emu beaks are slightly rounded, and not too hard.

Even without such journalistic privileges, a visit to a large zoological park such as San Diego's can give you an in-depth feel for the awesome variety of fascinating, whimsical, and wild creatures that evolution has created. And larger natural history museums often have exhibits showing a particular branch on the tree of life, with the transitional fossils from ancient times to the modern era for particular species.

Appendix A

Our Fishy Ancestors

When these exhibits go back in time far enough, you'll see that we, along with all land mammals, reptiles, and birds, inherited many of our genes from a common fishy ancestor. Given that unneeded characteristics often hang around through the eons, it is not surprising that at a certain early stage of our fetal development we are very similar to birds, other mammals, amphibians, and reptiles. All of us have gill slits and tails, and our embryos look quite similar.

During the middle stage of fetal development, a special combination of each of our genes becomes active, and the rest get turned off. For humans, the gill arches become the bones of our lower jaw, middle ear, and voice box, which permit us to hear and speak, a useful adaptation for humans in their environment; whereas fish retain them as gills, which they need to survive in their environment.

The Advantages of Understanding Evolution

All of modern medicine is based on predictions about how viruses, bacteria, fungi, and other disease-causing agents behave and mutate—and these predictions are based on evolutionary principles. Developing vaccines for the 2020–21 COVID-19 pandemic and updating them has depended on studying the evolutionary process of the coronavirus. Researchers study the histories of recessive disease-causing genes to control hereditary illnesses. Modern agriculture, animal husbandry, and environmental strategies—such as developing bacterial strains that decompose hazardous materials—and other scientific applications are also based on evolutionary predictions.

An Important Distinction

So far, this discussion has been about why we should and must accept evolutionary theory rather than Creationism or Intelligent Design as the factual explanation for life on Earth. But it is important to make a distinction here: It is not fair or appropriate to test religious texts by the same criteria we use to test scientific theories. Religion is best understood as the perception of, and reverence for, things that no known material definition can contain—things that must be described in the language of allegory, metaphor, and parable.

However, it *is* fair to test religious texts when these are presented as quasi-scientific knowledge to be taught in schools, rather than as metaphysical truths for reflection and meditation. And since Intelligent Design supporters and Creationists claim that their beliefs are knowledge and fact—a better form of science—it is fair to test those beliefs to see whether they fulfill the criteria for valid scientific theory.

They don't. Creationism has not been verified by physical evidence. In fact, geological, fossil, and DNA records contradict each of its central claims. Intelligent Design is not testable, because it is ultimately based on divine intervention, and no empirical test can prove whether or not God intervened directly in the formation of the human race. In the instances where Creationism and Intelligent Design have been used to make predictions, those predictions have been shown to be wrong.

Which Predictions Pass the Test?

Perhaps the best way to illustrate this point is to compare the competing explanations for our origins and why we are the way that we are: Intelligent Design and the Young-Earth Creationists versus the theory of evolution. We begin with the claims advanced by intelligent design. The first example below almost made it into a public-school district's curriculum. Then we'll look at the even more fundamentalist claims of the Young-Earth Creationists.

On the Origin of Species

Intelligent Design says

Life shows evidence of having been designed by an intelligent agent; it cannot be completely explained by natural causes. Some proponents of this idea, such as the Christian biochemist Michael Behe, argue that Intelligent Design doesn't require us to believe that the earth is less than ten thousand years old or that the biological processes of evolution don't exist. These advocates of Intelligent Design have no problem with most of modern evolutionary biology, physics, and astronomy, but instead focus exclusively on the question of whether some forms of life exhibit the effects of intelligent action. Behe, in particular, claims that a number of biochemical systems

Appendix A

have properties common to designed systems in our larger world, and so are likely to have been designed themselves.

In his 1996 book *Darwin's Black Box: The Biochemical Challenge to Evolution*, Behe gives numerous examples of microscopic chemical "machines" that are found in nature, such as the bacterial flagellum, which acts as a kind of outboard motor for bacteria to propel themselves. Flagella are made up of finely calibrated, interdependent parts. Behe claims such organisms are "irreducibly complex": If any one of the parts were missing from the system, the organism's motor couldn't function. Behe concludes that such organisms could not have evolved piecemeal from precursors, and therefore must have been created directly by God. As evidence, he points out that no one at the time of writing had found precursors to the systems he listed in his book.[65]

Oddly enough, Behe described some of these systems as having "Rube Goldberg–like" designs, because they were so haphazardly put together—not exactly a point in favor of Intelligent Design.

Not surprisingly, given the huge number of microbiologists at work in so many different fields, it took very little time for a number of them to identify precursors to the flagellum. Since then, several more of Behe's examples of supposedly irreducibly complex structures and processes have been falsified, and as microbiology continues to advance we presume that eventually all will be.

The Theory of Evolution says

The species were not designed—their variations emerged haphazardly; whatever worked is what stuck. The theory assumes that every species, and the organs, systems, and microorganisms of which they are made, emerged through natural selection. It predicts that precursors will exist for each organism, going back to the first primitive single-celled organisms and (eventually) extremophiles that formed in the extreme conditions of the cooling Earth.

Behe's "irreducibly complex" structures in organisms are not exceptions to natural selection. Fairly quickly, biologist David DeRosier demonstrated a bacterial precursor to the bacterial flagellum cited by Behe.[66] This organ had a different use (transmitting plagues, unfortunately) but it exhibited the characteristic "rod and drive shaft" found on the bacterial flagellum. Sometime in the past, a minor mutation that enabled this protoflagellum to rotate gave it a new function as a propeller, offering the resulting new organism a better chance of survival. The improved bacterium reproduced, and the "motor" was perpetuated.

When organisms mutate (which they do frequently), natural selection preserves the useful mutations and lets the mistakes die off. This is why we so often find evidence of haphazard, whatever-works, Rube Goldberg–like structures, rather than Intelligent Design. In fact, the more complex organisms become, the more their salient characteristics seem cobbled together by evolutionary chance.

The Evolution of RNA

A more recent entry in the "It is too complicated to have occurred naturally, therefore it must be Intelligent Design" lineage is a 2009 book by a leading figure in the movement, philosopher Stephen C. Meyer, titled *Signature in the Cell*. In it, Meyer claims that RNA must have been created by an intelligent designer because there is no way both of RNA's two key building blocks could have evolved simultaneously on a primitive Earth.[67]

In a review of the book for BioLogos.org, however, Christian geneticist Darrel Falk pointed out, "As he was writing these words, however, some elegant experiments were taking place at the University of Manchester that showed there is a way, a very feasible way that both building blocks could have been produced through natural processes."[68]

Meyer also claimed that no RNA molecule had ever been evolved in a test tube that could do more than join two building blocks together, which he described as another supposed "dead end" for evolutionary scientists.

However, while Meyer's book was in press, Gerald Joyce and Tracey Lincoln published an article in the February 27, 2009, issue of the journal *Science*, "in which they demonstrated that evolved-RNA can take on a second function, the all-important replication activity," Falk said. "In just 30 hours their collection of RNA molecules had grown 100 million times bigger through a replication process carried out exclusively by evolved RNA molecules. So, another dead-end pronouncement by Meyer was breached."

Falk concludes his review by stating, "If the object of the book is to show that the Intelligent Design movement is a scientific movement, it has not succeeded . . . The science of origins is not the failure [that Meyers purports] it to be. It is just science moving along as science does—one step at a time."

Appendix A

On the Origin of Humanity

Young-Earth Creationists say

About 6,000 years ago, God created the earth and made Adam out of dust and Eve out of one of Adam's ribs.
 —*summarized from the website "Answers in Genesis"*[69]

Evolutionary biologists say

According to the cosmological, geological, and fossil record, the earth is about 4.5 billion years old. The precise ways in which the very first life originated are still being debated and explored, but here is one scenario that many experts have advocated: As the planet began to cool, pools and eventually oceans of water began forming, and within them also formed the chemical structures we call amino acids—the building blocks of life. As the sun's rays infused these molecules with energy, the first primitive single-celled life emerged, about 3.8 billion years ago. From there, the evolutionary path is much easier to follow.

As the first cells replicated themselves, mutations appeared. When certain mutations created new organisms better able to survive and reproduce in their environment, those organisms' biological traits spread. This process, called natural selection, caused many more-complex species to emerge over time.

The first dinosaurs began appearing on Earth about 230 million years ago. Immensely powerful and enjoying an ideal climate and environment filled with their natural food, they ruled the animal kingdom for 165 million years. And then they disappeared. What happened? Geological evidence tells us that 65 million years ago, a huge asteroid struck the earth. The resulting cataclysms and their effects on the biosphere caused the dinosaurs and some 50 to 70 percent of the other plant and animal species of that era to die off. One byproduct of this mass extinction was that early mammals, small creatures whose insignificance as prey had allowed them to survive among the dinosaurs, began to grow larger and to play a more dominant role in the earth's ecosystems.

The fossil and DNA evidence further shows that roughly 7 million years ago the first primitive humans and apes diverged from a common primate ancestor. The apes ultimately evolved into gorillas, chimpanzees, orangutans, and bonobos. The human genus (*Homo*) also evolved into different species—at least a dozen—some of which became our direct ancestors.

Modern humans (*Homo sapiens sapiens*) emerged only 100,000 to 120,000 years ago. In that era, more than half a dozen human species inhabited the earth. Today there is just one human species, us, but we now know that the Neanderthals, who emerged in Asia and Europe, actually interbred with us at times, and many of us still share some of their genetic material and traits.

All the other hominids, including our direct precursors—*Homo sapiens idaltu* (from Ethiopia), *Homo rudolfensis* (from East Africa), *Homo erectus* (from East Asia), *Homo soloenis* (from the Indonesian island of Java), and *Homo floresiensis* (who came from the Indonesian island of Flores, grew to a maximum height of three feet, had stone tools, and hunted in groups), and *Homo denisova* (from Siberia)—are now extinct. Many of these species were not robust enough to thrive in the environments in which they evolved. But recent evidence suggests that others, especially the Neanderthals, who evolved in Asia and Europe, interbred with *Homo sapiens* and contributed to the evolution of our species.

The Cause of Disease, Suffering, and Death in the World

Young-Earth Creationists say

After God created Adam and Eve, he told them not to eat the fruit of the tree of the knowledge of good and evil. At that time, all creation was perfect and there was no disease, suffering, or death. Animals did not prey on each other, and Adam and Eve did not kill animals for food. They were all vegetarians, including lions and tigers and dinosaurs, which the Young-Earth Creationists believe were created at the same time as humans and all other life, about 6,000 years ago.
—*summarized from "Answers in Genesis"*[70]

Evolutionary biologists say

The fossil record shows conclusively that death and disease predate the appearance of *Homo sapiens* on Earth. Fossilized intestines of prehistoric carnivores, for example, contain traces of other animals—their prey. Death is a basic feature of the evolutionary process; without it, better-adapted forms of life would not emerge. Suffering was born when the first primitive pain-sensing cells evolved in early organisms. These mutations increased the survival rates of organisms by helping them to perceive damage-causing elements in their environment and escape or avoid them. They are the precursors of our own highly complex nervous systems. Pain is not a punishment from God; it is the mixed gift of evolution. We tend to think of it as negative because pain is, well, painful. However, organisms that experience pain are more likely to live and reproduce than those that do not. Pain tells us to take our hand off a hot surface, to come in from the cold, to call for help, to visit the doctor. Suffering helps us survive, and like all feeling, both complicates and deepens our experience of life.

Unintelligent Design

Of all the problems with Intelligent Design, its name is perhaps most problematic. As we saw above, when you get right down to the basics of how we higher organisms work, we're cobbled together pretty haphazardly. It is what one would expect based on the way evolution works. Take our eyes, for example.

Obviously, sight is a huge evolutionary advantage for survival. Through evolutionary processes, numerous forms of eyesight have emerged in various species in various environments through the eons. Studies of living creatures and fossils show us eyes corresponding to every stage of development of "sight," from light-sensitive eyespots in unicellular organisms, to a deepening pit that makes light sensing a bit sharper in flatworms, to the advanced, camera-like eye that humans share with other vertebrates.

Yet because they derive from such a long line of precursors, our human eyes are not only one of the most complex but also one of the least efficient examples of physiological "design." Surely a divine creator, devising creation's crowning glory, would have come up with a much more efficient, comprehensive, and elegant conception for that being's most important sense organ.

Yet consider some of these design flaws: In most invertebrates' eyes, the nerves and blood vessels are located behind the retina; in ours, they are on the retina's surface. This gives us a blind spot. In order for us to see, the light photons of the images that come in through our pupils must travel upside-down on a complex path to the sight-processing part of the brain, which then must turn the image right side up. This complex adaptation wouldn't have been necessary in an eye designed from the beginning to be perfect. Furthermore, our retinas are not very robust. They can be detached fairly easily by a fall, a blow, or even an especially rough roller-coaster ride. Before the development of current surgery techniques, a detached retina meant blindness for that eye.

Our eyes can detect only a very limited part of the electromagnetic spectrum—what *we* call visible light. So even with both retinas firmly in place, we're practically blind compared with the many birds, insects, and nocturnal mammals that can see a much wider part of that spectrum, which gives them numerous advantages, including better night vision. Leaf-tailed geckos have eyes that can see 350 times better than ours can in dim light; dragonflies have eyes that can detect colors, polarized light, and minor movement in dim light as well; golden eagles can perceive a rabbit on the ground from a mile away; and the giant squid's eyes have organs that produce enough light for it to see its prey in the dark ocean depths where it lives. For each of these species, a mutation somewhere in its ancestral heritage gave it an advantage that caused its eyes to evolve in a different way than ours, enabling it to successfully occupy a new niche in nature.

More Examples of Unintelligent Design

Humans begin maturing sexually almost a decade before their brain's frontal lobes have matured. This means they're much more likely than other animals to procreate before they're mature enough to be good parents. This makes no sense as an aspect of a deliberate design, especially from a God highly concerned with human sexual morality. Evolutionarily, however, it does make sense. Individuals whose sex drive develops early—ahead of their sense of caution—are much more likely to pass on their genetic material.

Furthermore, natural childbirth is often harrowing. And before the advent of modern medicine, there was a significant maternal mortality rate. The evolutionary advantages of bodies built to move on two legs and large brains housed in proportionally large heads were both traits reinforced by natural selection. They are not, however, the ideal combination for a birthing mother. If the human female reproductive system had been intelligently designed, one would expect a better mechanism to handle those big heads, making giving birth much less painful, less prone to cause tearing, and safer for both the mother and child.

Appendix A

Then there is the way we reproduce: As astrophysicist Neil deGrasse Tyson put it, "What's this going on between our legs? It is like an entertainment system designed in the middle of a sewer system! No intelligent designer would design it this way." Tyson also said, "We eat, drink, and breathe through the same hole in our body, guaranteeing a certain percent of us will choke to death every year—that's stupid design. Dolphins have separate holes, so why couldn't we?"[71]

Sex-Obsessed Design?

The God portrayed in the Bible favors strictly limited forms of human reproduction—a man could only have sex with his wife or concubine, and almost everything else that caused him to ejaculate was considered unclean or an abomination, including accidental nocturnal emissions (Lev 15:16–32). Nature, however, seems to favor virtually unlimited reproductive variety. Asexual reproduction, such as cloning, is especially widespread; it is used by single-celled organisms like bacteria, many plants and fungi, and some bugs and insects. Even some larger animals, such as hammerhead sharks, reproduce asexually when sexual reproduction is not an option.

The variety of asexual reproduction in nature is impressive until you look at the amazing range of sexual reproduction—countless adaptations, all fascinating, and many bizarre. This is just what you would predict of evolution, since sexual reproduction, involving two sets of genes, naturally results in significantly more genetic variation than cloning. Sexual reproduction is so critical in nature that many fish, gastropods (snails and the like), and plants can actually change their sex depending on whether there is a need in a population for more males or females. Then there is the vast category of transspecies sex, and even transkingdom copulation attempts, between plants and animals. Thousands of different orchid species have evolved central parts that resemble female versions of certain insects, and are pollinated by the male insects that try to mate with them.

Many, many books have been written on the sexual exuberance of nature, so we'll just give one particularly intriguing example: the argonaut (or paper nautilus, a kind of octopus). Those of you who remember King Missile's 1992 rock hit "Detachable Penis" may be surprised to learn that such a thing actually exists in nature. The male argonauts have a spiraling detachable male organ called a hectocotylus that stores up sperm and then leaves the octopus's body when it senses a female in the neighborhood. It swims to the female by following her pheromone trail in the water and then locks on and deposits the sperm. Unfortunately for the male, his "penis" doesn't swim back to him, and he dies shortly after mating, but then again, that's true of every species of octopus—the males all die within a few weeks after mating. The considerably larger female argonauts, on the other hand, like all female octopuses, live much longer, in order to care for their young. They are often found with several hectocotyli latched onto them. If you'd like to see this wondrous phenomenon in action, watch biologist Carin Bondar's June 2013 Ted Talk on sex in the wild.[72]

There are also entire books, such as Bruce Bagemihl's *Biological Exuberance: Animal Homosexuality and Natural Diversity*, written to address the tangential subject of diversity in animal sexual orientation—homosexuality, bisexuality, and transgender manifestations—and the evolutionary reasons for such behaviors.[73] Many of these "designs" do not seem particularly intelligent, either, but they are part of nature and they are fascinating.

It is not surprising that humans see design in nature—whether they attribute it to divine intervention or to evolution—because humans themselves are designers, and always have been. Generally, our attempts to directly mimic or even improve on nature in the past were inferior, since we didn't have billions of years to winnow out the working models that nature gave us. But that, too, is changing rapidly with the advent of super computers, artificial intelligence, nanotechnology, and more.

The Cradle of Humanity

Scientists believe that the shifting tectonic plates that created the East African Rift Valley also contributed to the ideal environment for the proliferation of life, giving us a unique window into the evolutionary history of humanity. The Rift's deep lakes and sheltered canyons created the conditions that first nurtured the ancestors of modern humans and then preserved their bones. A lot of legwork from archeologists and paleontologists mixed with helpful erosion and volcanic activity that protected this fossil treasure trove contributed to some significant discoveries in the area. Two of the most significant are "Turkana Boy," the 1.5-million-year-old hominid male discovered in Kenya, who bears a strong resemblance to us, but with a narrower pelvis; and "Lucy," the 3.2-million-year-old hominid female discovered in Ethiopia, who is the oldest almost intact hominid fossil. She looks nothing like us, but is clearly an early hominid.

Appendix A

In her July 5, 2021, opinion piece for *Scientific American*, back when the museums were first reopening, Allison Hopper suggested that it was a good time to introduce ourselves, and our children, to the original Black ancestors of all human beings.[74] She pointed out that a variety of hominids from the African continent were the ones who first invented tools, used fire, and invented languages and religions. She suggested that visiting exhibits about their contributions would be a beautiful way for us to honor them.

We heartily agree.

Appendix B

What About Miracles?

BELIEVERS WHO MAKE THE case for a supernaturally intervening God frequently point to miracles as proof. We, however, question whether the examples they cite are truly direct divine interventions that contradict the laws of nature. We are not convinced that God is located outside the natural order and steps in from time to time to perform such miracles.

Many people claim to have experienced miracles that contravened nature and so must have come from God. Among the most common are an unexpected cure or healing; a premonition or serendipitous event that helped them avoid a disaster or encounter good fortune; and good weather for a special occasion, even though bad weather was predicted.

The list goes on. In fact, those who are members of certain kinds of evangelical churches tend to see God intervening almost everywhere, and happily attribute any good thing that happens to "the Lord"—an appropriate title for an omnipotent being.

We in no way wish to diminish the spiritual experiences of such people. At the same time, we maintain that it is possible to experience god without a supernatural intrusion into the natural order as evidence of God's omnipotence. And that's as it should be: It allows the morally beneficial belief in something larger and higher than ourselves without the confounding moral problem of a supernaturally intervening deity.

It also allows belief to coexist with reason. Science is based on the regularity of the natural order. If God randomly suspended nature's laws

Appendix B

from time to time, then science as we know it would be impossible. We would never be sure whether irregularities in our data meant that God was setting aside natural laws on that occasion to work a miracle, or whether the problems should be attributed to a natural cause we hadn't considered, such as bad experimental design or inadequate instruments.

A few Christian denominations explain that God did perform miracles in biblical times but that the age of miracles has passed. Even if that were the case, our science and ethics would still be untenable; if the interventions and noninterventions of God were unpredictable and inexplicable in ancient times, they would still be so today, especially since they would imply that God could still intervene, but for some reason is choosing not to.

Millions of people claim they've seen or experienced miracles. Are they all wrong? In order to sort it out, we need to understand clearly the various ways God might act or speak. Are there any proofs of divine action that we can affirm today without having to negate evidence and scientific theory? Let us examine a few of the common experiences that people often claim as miracles. They will shed much light on the way God can and does work without violating the laws of nature.

What About Medical Miracles?

It is possible to affirm and understand medical "miracles" without setting aside natural causes. One of the most common reasons for unpredicted, "impossible" cures is the power of the human mind, which modern medicine consistently underestimates: the power of nurturing care, humor, love, and other traditional healing aids that involve the creative, connective energy that is present in all of us.

In fact, the known effects of the mind's beliefs are so common that when pharmaceutical companies attempt to get drugs approved by the U.S. Food and Drug Administration (FDA), they have to perform tests that take belief into account. In these tests, one group of patients is given the new drug for the disease they are trying to cure, and a control group gets a placebo that looks and tastes the same as the real pill but has no active ingredients. Neither the patients nor the doctors know which patients are getting the real pills and which are getting the placebos; only the researchers know. This is because a high percentage of people will get better just by taking a pill or receiving a treatment that they *think* will cure them. Interestingly, in these trials the group taking the placebo will often do better than the group on the "real" medicine, in which case (we trust), the FDA does not approve the drug.

It is unfortunate that these placebo trials have frequently been the only use Western medicine has made of the role the human mind plays in healing the human body. Many religions and non-Western medical practitioners capitalize on mind-body connections in working their cures. Such traditional treatments of the sick include anointing with oil, laying on hands, praying or meditating, "slaying in the spirit" (when a Pentecostal preacher touches a sick person on the forehead and the person falls back into the arms of waiting church members), special foods, herbal medicines, massages, "humor therapy," and other dramatic treatments or caring personal attentions that have a positive effect on patients.

When these actions are carried out within a spiritual or religious context, the experience is often intensified. We also know that the mind can have a negative impact on the body, and that distorted relationships, guilt, and depression can negatively affect our health. During a course of treatment, a really skilled medical practitioner will address a patient's underlying emotional and personal problems as well as physical illness.

Because of the interconnection of the body and the mind, body-based therapies and practices can also positively affect a patient's mind, with results that may seem miraculous. Centuries-old practices such as tai chi, aikido, dance, yoga, and meditation have been proven to be effective in helping to control chronic pain, alter mood disorders, and address post-traumatic stress disorders. In fact, significant aerobic exercise on a daily basis is often more useful than mood-altering drugs for treating mild depression. Exercise also improves brain functioning while decreasing weight gain and controlling diabetes, and provides other benefits as well.

The medical establishment is beginning to recognize that belief, spirituality, ambience, and caring attention can be vital to the healing process. In recent years many major healthcare providers have begun making adjustments to their design of hospitals, medical training, and standards of care to reflect this reality.

Kaiser Permanente, the largest private, nonprofit healthcare provider in the United States, has been building its new hospitals with green-design strategies, creating rooms with windows and plenty of space for family members and visitors, with communal healing gardens and meditation rooms, noise-reducing acoustics, and other comforting and peaceful patient-centered amenities. The data show that these new approaches have led to consistently faster healing times for patients, fewer complaints, and happier medical staff members as well.

Sometimes the results of these more holistic treatments and approaches *do* seem miraculous. But people use the word "miracle" in many different senses. Most use it to mean good, unusual, out of the ordinary, but still explainable by natural causes. You can use the word in this sense and still have a place to speak of god, rather than insisting that "real" miracles require supernatural divine intervention.

What About People Who Hear God's Voice?

Those who have been exposed to only one religious worldview naturally have a very intense and focused faith. They tend to believe no other religion could possibly be credible. Their own, on the other hand, through lifelong teaching and reinforcement, has come to seem intuitive and obvious. In the huge Hindu swaths of India, or the Muslim-majority regions of the Middle East, this is to be expected. But it often happens in multicultural America as well, in closed communities that act as religious cocoons. Amish settlements and Hasidic neighborhoods that cut themselves off from the surrounding modern culture are two examples of this phenomenon, and Pentecostal and evangelical "cocoons" are even more common.

In many of the more upscale megachurch communities, children are homeschooled or attend Christian institutions, the family's entire social life is tied up with the church, and the community's reading and media choices are almost all Christian or Christian-approved. If, in addition, church families run their own businesses, work in other Christians' businesses, or don't work outside of the home, they may have very little close contact with those of differing belief systems.

In secular society, someone who claims God is talking to him or her is usually considered delusional. But in these closed evangelical and Pentecostal communities, often connected with emotionally vibrant megachurches, God talks—not just to the pastors, but also to almost every member of the church. An intimate God who talks to them personally is something they take for granted. Phrases like "The Lord told me . . . ," "The Lord wanted us to . . . ," and "Praise the Lord for . . ." pepper their conversations, and are meant quite literally. The Lord so personally present to them is credited with every event in their lives.

What About Miracles?

If their athletic team wins a tournament, it is thanks to the Lord's help. If a loved one who has been struggling with terminal illness for a long time finally passes away, the Lord brought her home. If a family has a lot of children, even though the mother is clearly not equipped to deal with them, it is a blessing from the Lord. If rain is forecast on the day of a church picnic, and the sun comes out instead, it is the Lord. But if there's a drought and local farmers would have really appreciated rain, generally, these believers don't think the Lord is responsible; it is just normal weather patterns or, in some cases, Satan's work. On the other hand, there is also the possibility that the farmers failed to pray, for an omnipotent God would have provided rain had the farmers prayed for it—or else they did pray, and the Lord withheld the blessing for other reasons unsearchable by human wisdom.

Some believers in the personal, intimate Lord attribute all successes and perceived blessings to Him, their all-powerful Father, and attribute misfortunes to sin, to the devil, to the original fall when God cursed the earth, to nature (which is fallen), or to purposes unknown. They know this is the way things are because the Bible (the Word of the Lord) tells them so.

Clearly, for the most part, the people who believe this are perfectly normal. In fact, they are often intelligent, as well as loving and upright citizens. They practice good works, helping to support homeless shelters, orphanages, anti-child trafficking programs, tutoring services for low-income students, and so on. Their charitable programs usually have a strong evangelistic component, but that's to be expected, since they believe that people can only be saved through Jesus Christ, and that conversion is the ultimate charity.

Psychological anthropologist and Stanford professor T. M. Luhrmann wanted to understand how it was that such evangelicals could believe in a God who talked to them personally and intervened in every aspect of their lives. She spent more than two years attending weekly services at Vineyard Church in Chicago, as well as their local conferences and special worship sessions. She attended one of their weekly house groups for a year. She interviewed many members of the church about their experience of God. She was upfront with them about why she was involved, explaining that this was the way anthropologists study and understand a culture. Not surprisingly, she came to regard many of them as good friends.

She came to the conclusion that these evangelicals were "training the mind in such a way that they experienced part of their mind as the presence of God."[75] Even though they weren't aware of it, they were using proven techniques of modern psychotherapy, as well as ancient traditions of spiritual formation, to learn to pray in a way that led them to feel they were truly hearing God's voice and witnessing His power in their daily lives. Not surprisingly, those who had grown up immersed in this way of thinking took it for granted. But Luhrmann noticed that new converts had to work at it and often confessed frustration that they didn't feel God speaking to them as other church members did.

Because they were convinced that God is omnipotent, Vineyard members often wondered why God allowed them to suffer misfortunes and tragedies. One of Luhrmann's subjects felt deeply guilty because she thought her own lack of faith in prayer had contributed to another church member's miscarriage.

Such dilemmas go hand in hand with a strict traditional belief in God's omnipotence. The spiritual benefits devout Christians receive from practicing the presence of God in their daily lives are undeniable—it is an excellent practice for anyone.

The problem is the co-opting of the name "God." If you talk to these believers or listen to the media, you'll get the impression that unless you believe in this omnipotent, all-active God "you don't really believe in God at all." Inevitably, many do conclude that they can't believe in this version of God, and that they have no option but to give up on God and religion altogether and join the growing ranks of the "nones." That is unfortunate, because there are so many more credible and attractive ways of thinking about religion and the sacred (as this book explains, especially in Part II). Why should the narrowest and least believable concepts of God dominate our culture's ideas?

What if Christians felt able to practice the presence of god in a less dualistic way, one that does not set aside nature but is integrated with it? This, we suggest, might give them a better grasp of god and reality, and better equip them to deal with the sorrows that come from living in this world.

A couple with a severely disabled child might say, "God gave us Courtney because He knew we were strong enough to care for her." At first glance this attitude seems noble, loving, and devout. Clearly these are good people who trust the goodness and wisdom of their God. And yet looked at another way, it is disturbing: Are they actually attributing disabled children such as their daughter to this good, wise God; do they believe he caused their daughter's serious mental and physical afflictions in order to try her soul and theirs? Why Courtney, why them, when he accepts others' devotion without trying them so cruelly?

People of faith don't *have to* interpret events in this way, an interpretation that makes their loving God seem strangely harsh, even capriciously so. What if the couple really means something like this: "We are trying to interpret our lives as pervaded by the divine presence. We are trying to see everything as connected with God."

Imagine that they become increasingly aware of the nonliteral nature of their own religious language. They continue to talk as if God were the direct cause of (almost) every event, because that's their religious habit, but they are now able to recognize that much of this language is metaphorical. This less literal understanding enables them to feel that God is with them every moment, radiating love and sharing their sorrows, as they deal with the heartbreaking hardships that their daughter is facing. Isn't that a better place for them to be?

What About Premonitions?

Even people who don't regularly feel that God is talking to them will experience premonitions. If you pay attention to your premonitions—fleeting hopes or fears or expectations about the future—you will notice you have them often; everyone does. If you pay close attention, you will also notice that in the majority of cases, these premonitions don't come true, except in cases where you latch onto a realistic hope and actively (though perhaps unconsciously) work to make it happen.

Most people over a lifetime will experience very happy events and some tragic ones. For those who live in extraordinary circumstances—for example in a very privileged family, or conversely in a war zone or in a very poor, violent neighborhood—the odds of having unusually fortunate or tragic experiences are even higher. For everyone, chances are good that occasionally a fleeting thought—perhaps based on subconscious observation of the environment or people's faces—will be followed by a stroke of good fortune or a sudden danger or disaster that ties in with that thought. When that happens, we definitely take notice.

A certain kind of believer interprets these premonitions as messages from God. But what if God, who warned them of danger on one occasion, doesn't warn them on the next? Were they being judged that second time, because they weren't listening to God? Or were they simply in riskier or less familiar circumstances, or paying less attention to the people and objects around them?

It is appropriate to be thankful for premonitions that lead us to good fortune or save us from trouble. These kinds of experiences can bring us a wonderful sense of interconnectedness that we can equate with the divine presence. That is not the same thing, however, as believing literally that an omnipotent God has intervened to override the natural order on our behalf.

What About Miscellaneous Miracles That Seem Impossible to Explain by Natural Causes?

People do sometimes witness or experience events that seem impossible to explain by natural causes. Are they miracles? Or are they phenomena for which a natural explanation is not apparent, but does exist and will probably someday be found?

In the delightful novel *The Hummingbird's Daughter*, Luis Alberto Urrea wrote about his great-aunt Teresita.[76] She was acclaimed as a saint after she suffered a terrible assault that killed her, and then miraculously rose from the dead and became a healer. Thanks to modern medicine, we now know that she likely suffered an extended cataleptic episode, precipitated by the extreme shock of the assault, in which the body becomes rigid and unresponsive, and all bodily functions including breathing slow down to the point where they become indiscernible. In the late 1800s, her doctors were not aware of this phenomenon, and so Teresita's eventual recovery seemed like a miracle. (Fortunately, she was not buried before she revived!)

Science and medicine have advanced since then, but there is still plenty that has yet to be discovered. So, if you run into an apparently miraculous event, we suggest you inhabit your faith, acknowledge science, and sit with the tension. You may not yet know the full explanation. Gradually a beautiful process of dialogue develops, a process not unlike the way long-term partners create a community where one did not previously exist, not by erasing each other's former reality, but by keeping both in the mix. Let the language of faith and the language of science be what they are, and do not be afraid of the tension. There's beauty in the dialogue and in the questions.

Endnotes

Part One: Creation: What We Now Know

1. In Search of the Sacred

1. We (the coauthors) hear from evangelical leaders, even some who are among the most influential, that they estimate as many as half of the evangelical pastors they know no longer believe the traditional doctrines. Although they usually divulge this information in confidence, it is no longer a big secret in theological circles, even if it still is in much of the church. Some of these pastors eventually leave the church. Some move to mainline denominations. Some begin to bravely lead their flocks to struggle with these issues too, but often lose their job as a result. Others create atheist or secular alternatives to church. But for the vast majority of doubters in the evangelical clergy, their lack of faith is an uncomfortable secret to be kept from their flocks until they can retire (if they have a retirement plan).

2. In *Defense of "Spiritual,"* Sam Harris wrote a plea to his fellow skeptics and atheists to reclaim the word "spiritual" and put it to good use, using Christopher Hitchens and Carl Sagan to buttress his argument: https://samharris.org/a-plea-for-spirituality/.

2. In the Beginning . . .

3. Edward O. Wilson, *The Social Conquest of Earth* (New York: Liveright, 2012), 7–8.

Endnotes

3. We Are All Star-Stuff

4. Lord Martin Rees, in an interview that aired November 21, 2013, on *On Being with Krista Tippett*. https://onbeing.org/programs/martin-rees-cosmic-origami-and-what-we-dont-know.

5. Wikipedia, "List of space telescopes." https://en.wikipedia.org/wiki/List_of_space_telescopes (last edited on December 5, 2024, at 11:24 [UTC]).

6. Carl Sagan, *Pale Blue Dot: A Vision of the Human Future in Space* (New York: Random House, 1994), 50.

7. Brian Swimme, in "Comprehensive Compassion," a 2003 interview with Susan Bridle, *What Is Enlightenment*, issue 19 (now known as *Enlighten Next*), http://www.thegreatstory.org/SwimmeWIE.pdf.

4. The Dynamic Drive at Life's Core

8. For an extensive treatment of evolution and in-group loyalty, see Edward O. Wilson, *The Social Conquest of Earth* (New York: Liveright, 2012).

9. Connie Barlow, *The Ghosts of Evolution: Nonsensical Fruit, Missing Partners, and Other Ecological Anachronisms* (New York: Basic Books, 2000), quoted in Michael Dowd, *Thank God for Evolution!* (Chicago: Council Oaks, 2006), 130.

5. Our Big Brains & Why We Are the Way We Are

10. Jan Sleutels, "The Flintstones Fallacy," *Journal of Dialogue and Universalism*, 23.1 (January 2013): 65–75. ("Flintstones Fallacy" has also referred to the cartoon's portrayal of dinosaurs and humans living at the same time, in spite of the 65-million-year gap between the last dinosaurs and the first humans, but that is not the way Sleutels uses the term.)

11. See Matthew 26:41; Mark 14:38.

12. Daniel Goleman and Richard J. Davidson, *Altered Traits: Science Reveals How Meditation Changes Your Mind, Brain, and Body* (New York: Avery, 2017).

13. Jonathan Haidt, *The Happiness Hypothesis: Finding Modern Truth in Ancient Wisdom* (New York: Basic Books, 2006), 11. The original 2003 research is published in J. M. Burns and R. H. Swerdlow's "Right orbitofrontal tumor with pedophilia symptom and constructional apraxia sign," *Archives of Neurology* 60.3 (2003): 437–40.

14. Sam Harris, *Free Will* (New York: Free Press, 2012). For a more in-depth look at the concept of free will, see Philip Clayton's review of this book in *Inference: International Review of Science*, 1.2: https://inference-review.com/article/free-will-again; see also Philip Clayton and James W. Walters, ed., *What's with Free Will? Ethics and Religion after Neuroscience* (Eugene, OR: Cascade Books, 2020).

15. Roy F. Baumeister, E. J. Masicampo, and C. Nathan DeWall, "Prosocial Benefits of Feeling Free: Disbelief in Free Will Increases Aggression and Reduces Helpfulness," *Personality and Social Psychology Bulletin*, 35.2 (February 2009), 260–68, at: https://pubmed.ncbi.nlm.nih.gov/19141628.

16. David Sloan Wilson, *Evolution for Everyone: How Darwin's Theory Can Change the Way We Think about Our Lives* (New York: Delacorte, 2007), 70.

17. The famous phrase "Power tends to corrupt; absolute power corrupts absolutely" was written by Lord Acton in a letter to Bishop Creighton on April 5, 1887. See John Emerich Edward Dalberg Acton, *Historical Essays and Studies* (London: Macmillan, 1907).

18. For more on the so-called He Jiankui genome editing incident, please see Wikipedia, "He Jiankui genome editing incident," https://en.wikipedia.org/wiki/He_Jiankui_genome_editing_incident (last edited on December 21, 2024, at 22:39 [UTC]).

19. Edward O. Wilson, *The Social Conquest of Earth* (New York: Liveright, 2012), 7.

Part Two: Religion Comes of Age

6. Omnipresent God

20. See the apology from the *Harvard Icthus* here: https://harvardichthus.org/2013/11/an-apology.

21. Romans 8:28.

22. See "Lisa, a Case Study" in Monica A. Coleman, *Making a Way Out of No Way: A Womanist Theology*, Innovations: African American Religious Thought (Minneapolis: Fortress, 2008), 1–3, cf. 172–73.

23. See the blog post by James F. McGrath, https://www.patheos.com/blogs/religionprof/2018/03/why-i-am-a-panentheist.

24. Dr. Martin Luther King Jr.'s Christmas sermon from 1967, "Peace on Earth," is now available on Spotify: https://open.spotify.com/track/3mxz3RQMHOH4rpIccRjxPj.

7. Religion Comes of Age

25. A famous book that pokes fun in exactly these ways is David Hume, *Dialogues Concerning Natural Religion*, available online: https://www.gutenberg.org/files/4583/4583-h/4583-h.htm.

26. For more technical accounts of these views, see Philip Clayton, *The Problem of God in Modern Thought* (Grand Rapids: Eerdmans, 2000); and Philip Clayton, *God and Contemporary Science* (Grand Rapids: Eerdmans, 1997).

Endnotes

8. A Way to Hold Both Your Faith and Your Doubts

27. Jeffrey M. Jones, "U.S. Church Membership Falls Below Majority for First Time," https://news.gallup.com/poll/341963/church-membership-falls-below-majority-first-time.aspx, March 29, 2021.
28. Andrew Sullivan, "When Not Seeing Is Believing," *Time*, October 9, 2006, https://time.com/archive/6678673/when-not-seeing-is-believing.
29. Andrew Sullivan, "When Not Seeing Is Believing."
30. Matthew 19:9.

9. Holy Books and Miracles

31. M. Duris, J. Bjorck, and R. Gorsuch, "Christian Subcultural Differences in Item Perceptions of the MMPI-2 Lie Scale," *Journal of Psychology and Christianity* (Winter 2007): https://www.questia.com/library/journal/1P3-1492493811/christian-subcultural-differences-in-item-perceptions.
32. Deuteronomy 3; Deuteronomy 13:6–17; Joshua 6; Judges 21.
33. Exodus 22:20; Deuteronomy 13:13–19; 2 Kings 10:18–27; 2 Chronicles 15:12–13.
34. 1 Timothy 2:11–15.
35. Exodus 21:7–11.
36. Deuteronomy 21:18–21.
37. Mark 1:34.
38. Deuteronomy 28:15–24.
39. Leviticus 11: 9–12.
40. Leviticus 11:7; Isaiah 66:17.
41. Leviticus 20:13.
42. C. S. Lewis, *Mere Christianity* (1952; reprint, New York: HarperCollins, 2001), 51–52.
43. This famous quote from Rabbi Hillel the Elder can be found here: https://www.sefaria.org/Shabbat.31a.5?lang=en.
44. Cynthia Bourgeault's introduction to *The Gospel of Mary*, in *The Luminous Gospels: Thomas, Mary Magdalene, and Philip*, edited and translated by Lynn C. Bauman, Ward J. Bauman, and Cynthia Bourgeault (Telephone, TX: Praxis, 2008), 56.

10. The Afterlife

45. Sam Parnia, *Erasing Death: The Science That Is Rewriting the Boundaries Between Life and Death* (New York: HarperCollins, 2014). See Dr. Parnia's more recent book, *Lucid Dying: The New Science Revolutionizing How We Understand Life and Death* (New York: Grand Central, 2024).

46. Michael Shermer, *Why People Believe Weird Things: Pseudoscience, Superstition, and Other Confusions of Our Time* (New York: Freeman, 1997), 78.
47. Shermer, *Why People Believe Weird Things*, 79.
48. See for example Matthew 13:42, 50.
49. Rob Bell, *Love Wins* (San Francisco: HarperOne, 2012), 72.
50. See Luke 16:19–30.
51. Rob Bell, *Love Wins* (San Francisco: HarperOne, 2012), 73.
52. This speech by Sam Harris is now available here: https://www.tiktok.com/@atheist.archive/video/7311467147325328686.

11. Science, Religion, and Sacred Stories

53. Many studies show that greater gender equality makes for more peaceful, democratic, prosperous, and environmentally sustainable societies. These studies include the United Nations Development Program's "Powerful Synergies: Gender Equality, Economic Development, and Environmental Sustainability," September 27, 2012: https://www.undp.org/content/undp/en/home/librarypage/womens-empowerment/powerful-synergies. See also Gérard Tchouassi, "Does Gender Equality work for Sustainable Development in Central Africa Countries? Some Empirical Lessons," *European Journal of Sustainable Development* (2012): 383–98: https://ecsdev.org/ojs/index.php/ejsd/article/view/25/19.
54. Lauren Hall, quoted in the *New York Times* article by Kate Zernike, "Five Women Sue Texas Over the State's Abortion Ban," November 6, 2023: https://www.nytimes.com/2023/03/06/us/texas-abortion-ban-suit.html.
55. Joanna Grossman is quoted in María Méndez, "Texas Laws Say Treatments for Miscarriages . . . ," *Texas Tribune*, July 20, 2022: https://www.texastribune.org/2022/07/20/texas-abortion-law-miscarriages-ectopic-pregnancies.
56. See Pope Francis's *Laudato si* (2015): https://www.vatican.va/content/francesco/en/encyclicals/documents/papa-francesco_20150524_enciclica-laudato-si.html, and Francis's "Laudate Deum": Apostolic Exhortation to all people of good will on the climate crisis (2023): https://www.vatican.va/content/francesco/en/apost_exhortations/documents/20231004-laudate-deum.html.
57. Quoted in Michael Dowd, *Thank God for Evolution!* (Chicago: Coucil Oak, 2006), 7.

12. Our Sacred Story: Two Visions

58. See for example Loriliai Biernacki and Philip Clayton, eds., *Panentheism across the World's Traditions* (New York: Oxford University Press, 2013).
59. See the YouTube link to the video of Neil deGrasse Tyson speaking to a group of scientists and educators gathered at a Science Network conference at the Salk Institute in San Diego, CA, in November 2006: https://www.youtube.com/watch?v=bcTbGsUWzuw.

60. See Becka A. Alper, "How Religion Intersects with Americans' Views of the Environment," Pew Research Center Report, November 17, 2022: https://www.pewresearch.org/religion/2022/11/17/how-religion-intersects-with-americans-views-on-the-environment.

Appendix A: Creative Emergence or Intelligent Design?

61. Phil Zuckerman, *Society Without God* (New York: New York University Press, 2008).
62. Greg Epstein, *Good Without God* (New York: Morrow, 2009).
63. This statement was made at a public meeting. Similar claims are made, for example, by writers at the Institute for Creation Research. See e.g. Duane Gish, "As a Transitional Form Archaeopteryx Won't Fly," https://www.icr.org/article/321.
64. Wikipedia, "Evolution of birds," https://en.wikipedia.org/wiki/Evolution_of_birds (last edited on December 11, 2024, at 12:13 [UTC]).
65. Michael J. Behe, *Darwin's Black Box* (New York: Free Press, 1996).
66. David DeRosier refutes Michael Behe's claim during the trial covered by *Nova* for PBS in this segment: www.pbs.org/wgbh/nova/evolution/intelligent-design-trial.html.
67. Stephen C. Meyer, *Signature in the Cell* (New York: HarperOne, 2010).
68. Darrel Falk, "Signature in the Cell," *Biologos* (blog), December 28, 2009: https://biologos.org/articles/signature-in-the-cell. The following examples in the text are drawn from Falk's excellent article.
69. See https://www.AnswersInGenesis.org.
70. AnswersInGenesis.org.
71. Neil deGrasse Tyson, speaking to a group of scientists and educators gathered at a Science Network conference at the Salk Institute in San Diego, CA, in November 2006: https://www.youtube.com/watch?v=bcTbGsUWzuw.
72. Carin Bondar's Ted Talk on sex in the wild, June 2013: https://www.ted.com/talks/carin_bondar_the_birds_and_the_bees_are_just_the_beginning.
73. Bruce Bagemihl, *Biological Exuberance*, illustrated by John Megahan (New York: St. Martin's, 1999).
74. Allison Hopper, "Denial of Evolution Is a Form of White Supremacy," *Scientific American*, July 5, 2021: https://www.scientificamerican.com/article/denial-of-evolution-is-a-form-of-white-supremacy.

Appendix B: What about Miracles?

75. T. M. Luhrmann, *When God Talks Back: Understanding the American Evangelical Relationship with God* (New York: Knopf, 2012).
76. Luis Alberto Urrea, *The Hummingbird's Daughter: A Novel* (New York: Little, Brown, 2005).

www.ingramcontent.com/pod-product-compliance
Lightning Source LLC
Chambersburg PA
CBHW020848160426
43192CB00007B/839